TOEFL 托福考试官方指南解析

金鑫 编著

北京语言大学出版社
BEIJING LANGUAGE AND CULTURE UNIVERSITY PRESS

图书在版编目(CIP)数据

托福考试官方指南解析 / 金鑫编著. —北京：北京语言大学出版社，2013.6

ISBN 978-7-5619-3527-9

Ⅰ.①托… Ⅱ.①金… Ⅲ.①TOEFL—自学参考资料

Ⅳ.①H310.41

中国版本图书馆 CIP 数据核字（2013）第 121946 号

书 名：托福考试官方指南解析
著 者：金 鑫
责任编辑：李 亮 张 茜
封面设计：大愚设计+代玲玲

出版发行：北京语言大学出版社
社 址：北京市海淀区学院路 15 号 邮政编码：100083
网 站：www.blcup.com
电 话：发行部 (010)62605588 /5019 /5128
编辑部 (010)62418641
邮购电话 (010)62605127
读者服务信箱 bj62605588@163.com
印 刷：北京海石通印刷有限公司
经 销：全国新华书店

版 次：2013 年 7 月第 1 版 2013 年 7 月第 1 次印刷
开 本：787 毫米×1092 毫米 1/16 印张：15.5
字 数：178 千
书 号：ISBN 978-7-5619-3527-9
定 价：35.00 元

前言

托福考试是进入国外大学深造的敲门砖，优秀的托福成绩会为我们进入理想的学校提供更多的机会。作为一名从业十年的托福老师，我一直和广大托福考生一起奋斗在备考的第一线，也一直在尽最大的努力通过自己托福教学的经验帮助更多的学生进入世界名校。

《托福考试官方指南》（*The Official Guide to the TOEFL Test*，简称OG）作为托福考试唯一命题中心ETS出版的权威指南，在学生的考试准备过程中起着举足轻重的作用。但是，OG中对考试的介绍只是提纲挈领的，对于题目的解析也比较简单，没有系统性、规律性的题型归类和解题方法，也没有专门适合中国考生的备考指导和答题技巧。对于考生来说，这无疑是个很大的缺憾。为了满足这个需求，这是我第二次为OG做出全方位的深度解析，与旧版解析不同的是，本书针对OG里面所出现的文章与题目给予了更加详细的解释，并增加了新版OG中新增内容的剖析。本书紧抓ETS命题思路，致力于帮助考生更好地掌握托福考试的答题方法以及理解问题的角度，在备考的过程中少走弯路。

听力部分中，OG中每一道听力题目都有详细的解析。解题关键句在听力原文中进行标注，并和正确答案一一对应，以相当直观的形式呈现出来，简洁明了，同时辅以中文解答，帮助考生训练在听力过程中捕捉重点信息的能力。“听力思路与考点总结”列举出关键性的、规律性的词句，需要在听力过程中重点关注，对后面的解题有重要的提示作用，往往是考点所在。

阅读部分中，OG中每一篇阅读文章同样都配有精细的讲解。每篇文章都给出了文章结构框架和重点词汇，能够对理解文章内容和解题起到有效的辅助作用。书中对题目进行了归类，并总结了各类题型的经典解题方法；考生可以将这些方法推而广之，应用到具体的解题当中。此外，关键词和定位句将题目和原文建立起直接的对应联系，解题思路实用又简捷，同时总结了正确选项和错误选项的特征，帮助考生提高解题速度。

本书是理论大纲和实战经验的结晶，是浓缩的精华，相信对考生备考托福有核心的指导性作用。不过需要说明的一点是，本书没有包含口语和写作两部分，主要是因为这两部分属于语言输出性题目，非一日之功，不是学习一些纯粹的技能就能提高的，建议考生通过吸收大量的语料来提高口语和写作能力。本书中不再赘述。

人生最幸福的事情就是为了梦想而奋斗，而托福考试是我们触及梦想的第一步。只有在理解了考试命题思路的同时，运用恰当的方法，才能获得最终的成功。我希望通过阅读这本书，考生能够在深入了解托福考试的基础上，有效改善逻辑思维能力，这种能力的培养对进入国外学校继续深造有着深远的意义。

很感谢一直以来支持与关爱我的同事们和朋友们、感谢我的学生们，正是你们促使我在托福教学的道路上不断地努力、不断地进步。

亲爱的考生朋友，如果你对某些题目或者某些方法有进一步的见解与想法，欢迎随时和我联系。祝你们都考出好成绩，早日进入自己理想的学校！

编　者

目 录

TOEFL iBT Listening（听力部分）

Listening Practice Sets

Authentic TOEFL Practice Test 1

Authentic TOEFL Practice Test 2

Authentic TOEFL Practice Test 3

TOEFL iBT Reading（阅读部分）

Reading Practice Sets

Authentic TOEFL Practice Test 1

Authentic TOEFL Practice Test 2

Authentic TOEFL Practice Test 3

TOEFL iBT LISTENING

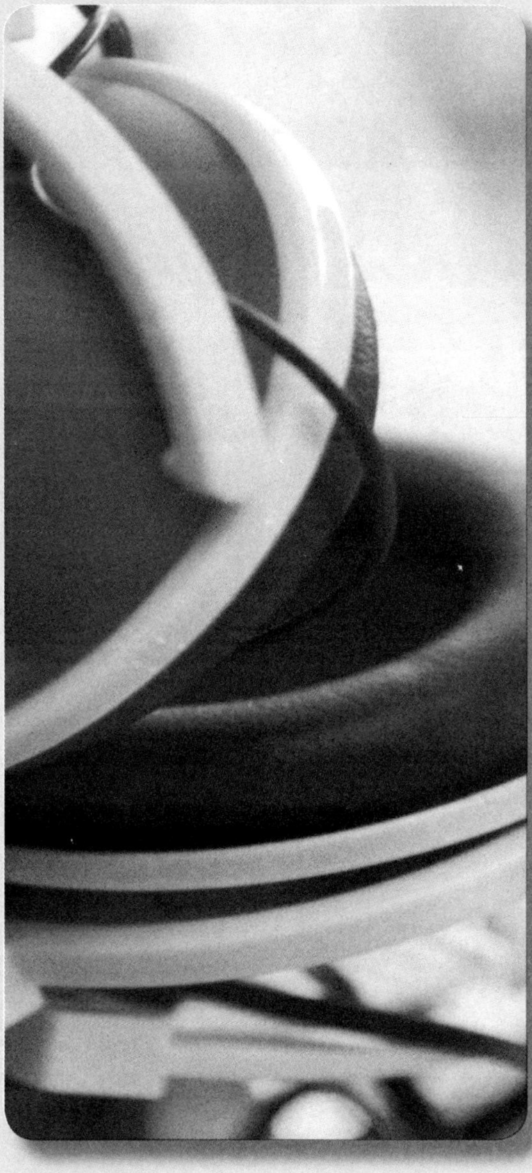

托福考试官方指南解析

听 力 部 分

Listening Practice Sets

Practice Set 1

对话 || 关于气象变化的论文写作

题目解析

1

Why does the man go to see his professor?

(A) To ~~borrow~~①some charts and graphs② from her

(B) To ask her to explain some ~~statistical procedures~~

(C) To talk about a report he is writing

(D) To discuss ~~a grade~~ he got on a paper

Professor

Sure, John. What did you wanna talk about?

Student

Well, I have some quick questions about how to write up the **research project** I did this semester—about climate variations.

选项(A)，①对话中未提到过任何关于“borrow...”的信息，故此选项错误。②“charts and graphs”都是细节信息，不能成为主旨题的正确选项。

选项(B)中的“statistical procedures”这个概念对话中并未提及。对话中提到的是“statistical tests”，且属于细节信息，故不是正确答案。

选项(D)中的“grade”是对话中未提及的内容，一定错误。

听力技巧：在听力部分，ETS经常用原文中并未出现的一些信息作为题目的迷惑选项，此类选项必错。该类选项中未被提及的内容在以下题目中均已用删除线标明，以后不再重复说明。

2

Listen again to part of the conversation. Then answer the question.

Why does the professor say this?

(A) To question the ~~length of the paper~~

(B) To offer encouragement

(C) To dispute the data sources

(D) To explain ~~a theory~~

Professor

You know, you have to remember now that you're the expert on what you've done. So, think about what you'd need to include if you were going to explain your research project to someone with general or casual knowledge about the subject, like...like your parents. That's usually my rule of thumb: would my parents understand this?

Student

OK. I get it.

Professor

I hope you can recognize by my saying that how much you do know about the subject.

由"You know, you have to remember now that you're the expert on what you've done. So, ..."这两句话我们可以知道，教授所要强调的是学生要有信心，把自己当做该课题的研究专家，然后考虑报告里到底还应该加一些什么内容。因此，在教授说"I hope you can recognize by my saying that how much you do know about the subject"这句话时，仍然是要强调她所表达的中心意思。只有选项(B)的内容与此相关，故正确。

(A)(D)两选项中删除线所标内容在对话中完全未提及，故教授说话的目的不可能与这两项的内容相关。选项(C)中的data sources是对话中间部分提及的内容，而本题考点出现在前半部分，此内容位置与考点位置不对应，因此不能成为本题的正确答案。

3

What information will the man include in his report?

Climate charts (**include**)

Interviews with meteorologists (**not include**)

Journal notes (**include**)

Statistical tests (**include**)

Student

Right. I understand. I was wondering if I should also include the notes from the research **journal** you suggested I keep?

Professor

Yes, definitely. You should use them to indicate what your evolution in thought was through time. So, just set up, you know, what was the purpose of what you were doing—to try to understand the climate variability of this area—and what you did, and what your approach was.

Student

OK. So, for example, I studied meteorological records; I looked at **climate charts**; I used different methods for analyzing the data, like certain statistical tests; and then I discuss the results. Is that what you mean?

Professor

Yes, that's right. You should include all of that. The **statistical tests** are especially important. And also be sure you include a good reference section where all your published and unpublished data came from, 'cause you have a lot of unpublished climate data.

本题是对细节信息的考查。

4

Why does the professor tell the man about the appointment at the doctor's office?

(A) To demonstrate a way of remembering things

(B) To explain why she needs to ~~leave soon~~

(C) To ~~illustrate a point that appears in his report~~

(D) To emphasize ~~the importance of good health~~

Student

= forgetful

Hmm...**something just came into my mind and went out the other side**.

Professor

That happens to me a lot, **so I've come up with a pretty good memory management tool**. I carry a little pad with me all the time and jot down questions or ideas that I don't want to forget. **For example, I went to the doctor** with my daughter and her baby son last week, and we knew we wouldn't remember everything we wanted to ask the doctor, so we actually made a list of five things we wanted answers to.

首先请注意一个表达：Something just came into my mind and went out the other side = forgetful。学生说“我总是记不住事情”，对此教授解释道“这种事也经常发生在我身上，所以我想出一个非常好的记忆管理方法。我总是带一个小便签本，把我不想忘的问题和想法随手写下来。比如说，上次我陪我的女儿和她的小孩去看医生……”因此，教授提到去看医生的目的是为了说明一种防止忘记事情的方法，即把事情写在便签本上。选项(A)正确。

5

What does the professor offer to do for the man?

(A) ~~Help him collect more data~~ in other areas of the state

Student

Yes. It ends up that I have data on more than just the immediate Grant City area, so I also included some regional data in

(B) Submit his research findings for publication

(C) Give him the doctor's telephone number

(D) Review the first version of his report

the report. With everything else it should be a pretty good indicator of the climate in this part of the state.

Professor

Sounds good. I'd be happy to **look over a draft version** before you hand in the final copy, if you wish.

Student

Great. I'll plan to get you a draft of the paper by next Friday. Thanks very much.

请注意两组同义表达：look over = review; draft version = first version

听力思路及考点总结

1. Uh, excuse me, Professor Thompson. I know your office hours are tomorrow, but I was wondering if you had a few minutes free now to discuss something.

   ★ But之后的内容往往是考点。

   ★ I was wondering if之后的内容要注意听，往往是考点。

2. Sure, John. What did you wanna talk about?

   这种疑问句后的内容要注意听。原文中对这个疑问句的回答是第一题的正确答案。

3. Yes, that's right. You should include all of that. The statistical tests are especially important.

   ★ "You should..." 是一种典型的建议句型。建议句型在听力中出现时，往往成为考点。

   常考到的建议句型还有：

   Have you done...?

You might (also)...

If I were you (in your shoes), I would...

It doesn't hurt if you do...

Why not do...?

★ "...are especially important." 这种句子一定要听清楚，它本身就在强调这个内容是重要的，必为考点。

4. I'd be happy to look over a draft version before you hand in the final copy, if you wish.
在这种句型中，"if you wish" 之前的内容经常成为考点。

讲座 ‖ 哲学·古希腊哲学家亚里士多德的伦理理论——快乐

题目解析

1

What is the main purpose of the lecture?

(A) To illustrate the importance of <u>extrinsic values</u>

(B) To explain Aristotle's views about the importance of <u>teaching</u>

(C) To explain why people change what they value

(D) To discuss Aristotle's views about human happiness

OK. Another ancient Greek philosopher we need to discuss is Aristotle—Aristotle's ethical theory. What Aristotle's ethical theory is all about is this: **he's trying to show you how to be happy—what true happiness is.** Now, Why is he interested in human happiness? It's not just because it's something that all people want or aim for. It's more than that. But to get there, we need to first make a very important distinction. Let me introduce a couple of technical terms: extrinsic value and intrinsic value.

教授先讲extrinsic value 和 intrinsic value的区别，目的是为了解释之后的主题happiness。整个讲座都是围绕着happiness这个主题进行的，故本题答案为选项(D)。

选项(A) ...extrinsic values和选项(B) ...teaching均为讲座中的细节信息，不可以成为主旨题的正确答案。

2

The professor gives examples of things that have value for her. Indicate for each example what type of value it has for her.

Teaching **(Intrinsic)**

Exercise **(Extrinsic)**

Health **(Both Extrinsic and Intrinsic)**

Playing a musical instrument **(Intrinsic)**

Exercise. There may be some people who value exercise for itself, but I don't. I value exercise because if I exercise, I tend to stay healthier than I would if I didn't. So I desire to engage in exercise, and **I value exercise extrinsically**...not for its own sake, but as a means to something beyond it. It brings me good health.

Health. Why do I value good health? Well, here it gets a little more complicated for me. Um, health is important for me because I can't...do other things I wanna do—play music, teach philosophy—if I'm ill. So health is important to me—has value to me—as a means to a productive life. But health is also important to me because I just kind of like to be healthy—it feels good. It's pleasant to be healthy, unpleasant not to be. So to some degree I value health both for itself and as a means to something else: productivity. **It's got extrinsic and intrinsic value for me.**

Then there's some things that are just valued for themselves. I'm a musician, not a professional musician; I just play a musical instrument for fun. Why do I value playing music? Well, like most amateur musicians, **I only play because, well, I just enjoy it. It's something that's an end in itself.**

Teaching → Intrinsic

Now, something else I value is teaching. Why? Well, it brings in a modest income, but I could make more money doing other things. I'd do it even if they didn't pay me. I just enjoy teaching. **In that sense it's an end to itself.** But teaching's not something that has intrinsic value for all people—and that's true generally...

在做本题时，除了以上被标明的几句话之外，大家应该注意一些核心意思在讲座中的重复，与itself alone，for its own sake意思相关的全属于intrinsic value；与not for itself，as a means to something else意思相关的全属于extrinsic value。

3

Why is happiness central to Aristotle's theory?

(A) Because it is so difficult for people to attain

(B) Because it is valued for its own sake by all people

(C) Because it is a means to a productive life

(D) Because most people agree about what happiness is

So how does all this relate to human happiness? Well, Aristotle asks: **is there something that all human beings value... and value only intrinsically, for its own sake and only for its own sake?** If you could find such a thing, that would be the universal final good, or truly the ultimate purpose or goal for all human beings. Aristotle thought the answer was yes. What is it? **Happiness**. Everyone will agree, he argues, **that happiness is the ultimate end to be valued for itself and really only for itself**. For what other purpose is there in being happy? What does it yield? The attainment of happiness becomes the ultimate or highest good for Aristotle.

教授讲extrinsic value 和 intrinsic value的区别是为了引出人们只用intrinsic value衡量的事物——happiness。所以此题选(B)。

选项(A)的内容在讲座中未提及。选项(C)中的productive life确实曾被提及，不过是在衡量health时提到的，出现在本题考点内容之前，与本题考点位置不对应。选项(D)完全错误，教授在提到what is happiness这个话题时指明了 people disagree。

4

According to the professor, why does Aristotle think that fame cannot provide true happiness?

(A) Fame cannot be obtained without help from other people.

(B) Fame cannot be obtained ~~by all people~~.

(C) Fame does not ~~last forever~~.

(D) People cannot ~~share~~ their fame with other people.

And, second, true happiness should be something that I can obtain on my own. I shouldn't have to rely on other people for it. Many people value fame and seek fame. Fame for them becomes the goal. But, according ~~to Aristotle, this won't work~~ either, **because fame depends altogether too much on other people. I can't get it on my own, without help from other people.**

此题答案在讲座中已经明确给出。正确答案为选项(A)。

5

Listen again to part of the lecture.

Then answer the question.

What does the professor mean when she says this?

Now, something else I value is teaching. Why? **Well, it brings in a modest income, but I could make more money doing other things.**

(A) Teaching is not a highly valued profession in society.

(B) She may change professions in order to earn more money.

(C) The reason she is a teacher has little to do with her salary.

(D) More people would become teachers if the salary were higher.

教授在讲她自己喜欢教学，她value teaching intrinsically，即：对教学的评价不受其他因素的影响。并且，教授说“虽然教学能给我带来不错的收入，但如果我做其他的工作，可以赚更多的钱”。这表明收入并不是她喜欢教学的原因。选项(C)指明了这一点，故正确。

听力思路及考点总结

1. Another ancient Greek philosopher we need to discuss is Aristotle—Aristotle's ethical theory. What Aristotle's ethical theory is all about is this: he's trying to show you how to be happy—what true happiness is.

   “Another...we need to discuss is...”这是引出文章主旨的一种表达方法，常常用来回答主旨题。

2. Why is he interested in human happiness? It's not just because...

   “It's not just because...”这句话中有明确的否定词，不用仔细听，但需要注意听它的真正原因是什么，即“it is because...”。一般情况下，听力中有明确否定词的地方，一般不会成为考点，不用认真听。但要注意与之相对应的肯定句所在的地方。此外，若听力中出现neither, hardly, doubt这类词时，要注意这些词所在的句子，它们虽然是肯定的形式，但实际上却表示否定，如“I could hardly wait”表达的意义是“我等不及了”。这些词所在的句子往往成为考点。

3. Let me introduce a couple of technical terms: extrinsic value and intrinsic value.

"Let me..."引导的内容需要认真听，它是说话者所要强调的内容，容易成为考点。

4. Why do I value playing music? Well, like most amateur musicians, I only play because, well, I just enjoy it. It's something that's an end in itself.

这是一个自问自答式的表达，往往有考点出现。听清问题后，只需要听出主要答案，对于答案的具体解释稍加注意即可，因为考点通常是这个主要答案，并不是对它的具体解释。题目中，教授的提问会成为最终的问题，而这个主要答案就是这道题的正确选项。

讲座 ‖ 心理学·行为理论

题目解析

1
━━━●

What is the professor mainly discussing?

(A) The development of ~~motor skills~~ in children

(B) How psychologists measure <u>muscle activity in the throat</u>

(C) A theory about the relationship between muscle activity and thinking

(D) A study on <u>deaf people's</u> problem-solving techniques

"Thinking can be measured as muscle activity"这个观点在讲座中被反复提及，故本主旨题的正确选项为(C)。

选项(A)中motor skill是讲座中从未提及的内容，必错。选项(B)中muscle activity in the throat和选项(D)中deaf people都是细节信息，不能成为主旨题的正确答案。

> 听力技巧：若在整篇文章中被反复提及的内容在主旨题的选项中出现，则该选项为正确答案。

2

Listen again to part of the lecture.

Then answer the question.

Why does the professor say this?

(A) To give an example of a laryngeal habit

(B) To explain the meaning of a term

(C) To explain why he is discussing laryngeal habits

(D) To remind students of a point he had discussed previously

Watson thought laryngeal habits—**you know, from *larynx*; in other words, related to the voice box**—he thought those habits were an expression of thinking.

“...in other words...”这个表达表明教授一定是要解释刚刚提到的术语或问题。考生必须熟记。与此功能相似的表达还有I mean...，that is (to say)...，Let’s put it this way...等。在讲座中，教授提到了“laryngeal habits”这个术语，这句话的出现表明教授接下来要解释这个术语，故选项(B)正确。

若出现“Oh, no. Wait a minute...”这种表达则表明说话者说错了话，他/她要更正这个错误。若出现“Tell me about it”或“You can say that again”这种表达则表明说话者同意前一个说话人的观点。

3

What does the professor say about people who use sign language?

(A) It is ~~not possible~~ to study their thinking habits.

(B) They exhibit laryngeal habits.

(C) The muscles in their hands move when they solve problems.

(D) They do not exhibit ideomotor action.

Student

Professor Blake, um, did he happen to look at people who sign? I mean deaf people?

Professor

Uh, he did indeed, um, and to jump ahead, what one finds in deaf individuals who use sign language when they’re given problems of various kinds, **they have muscular changes in their hands** when they are trying to solve a problem...**muscle changes in the hand**, just like the muscular changes going on in the throat region for speaking individuals.

本题是对细节信息的考查，选项(C)与原文意思完全对应，故正确。注意本题出题点的设置，位于讲座中“问题—回答”的地方，即有问有答之处。上文讲过，这种位置经常是考点。

选项(D)中的ideomotor action是在此内容之后提到的，出现在本题考点位置之后，与本题考点位置不对应，故错误。

4

What point does the professor make when he refers to the university library?

(A) A study on problem solving took place there.

(B) Students should go there to read more about behaviorism.

(C) Students' eyes will turn toward it if they think about it.

(D) He learned about William James's concept of thinking there.

Ideomotor action is an activity that occurs without our noticing it, without our being aware of it. I'll give you one simple example. **If you think of locations, there tends to be eye movement that occurs with your thinking about that location.** In particular, from where we're sitting, imagine that you're asked to think of our university library. Well, if you close your eyes and think of the library, and if you're sitting directly facing me, then according to this notion, **your eyeballs will move slightly to the left, to your left, 'cause the library's in that general direction.**

教授提到图书馆这个例子就是为了说明“If you think of locations, there tends to be eye movement that occurs with your thinking about that location”（如果你在想某个地方，你的眼球就会转向那个方位）这句话。所以当学生们想着图书馆时，他们的眼球会转向图书馆的方向。故选项(C)正确。

5

The professor describes a magic trick to the class. What does the magic trick demonstrate?

(A) An action people make that they are not aware of

(B) That behaviorists are ~~not really scientists~~

(C) How psychologists ~~study children~~

(D) A method for ~~remembering locations~~

Ideomotor action is an activity that occurs without our noticing it, without our being aware of it. I'll give you one simple example. If you think of locations, there tends to be eye movement that occurs with your thinking about that location. In particular, from where we're sitting, imagine that you're asked to think of our university library. Well, if you close your eyes and think of the library, and if you're sitting directly facing me, then according to this notion, your eyeballs will move slightly to the left, to your left, 'cause the library's in that general direction.

James and others said that **this is an idea leading to a motor action, and that's why it's called "ideomotor action"—an idea leads to motor activity**. If you wish to impress your friends and relatives, you can change this simple process into a magic trick. Ask people to do something such as I've just described: think of something on their left; think of something on their right. You get them to think about two things on either side with their eyes closed, and you watch their eyes very carefully. And if you do that, you'll discover that you can see rather clearly the eye movement—that is, you can see the movement of the eyeballs. Now, then you say, "Think of either one and I'll tell which you're thinking of."

教授用两个例子（例1：当学生们想到图书馆时，他们的眼球会不自觉地转向图书馆的方向。例2：学生们可以去给别人变一个小魔术magic trick）支持同一个观点“Ideomotor action is an activity that occurs without our noticing it, without our being aware of it.”只有选项(A)指出了这个例子要说明的问题。

6

What is the professor's opinion of the motor theory of thinking?

(A) Most of the evidence he has collected ~~contradicts~~ it.

(B) It explains adult behavior ~~better than~~ it explains child behavior.

(C) It is ~~the most valid~~ theory of thinking at the present time.

(D) It cannot be completely proved or disproved.

OK. Well, Watson makes the assumption that muscular activity is equivalent to thinking. But given everything we've been talking about here, one has to ask: are there alternatives to this motor theory—this claim that muscular activities are equivalent to thinking? Is there anything else that might account for this change in muscular activity, other ~~than saying that~~ it is thinking? And the answer is clearly yes. **Is there any way to answer the question definitively? I think the answer is no.**

教授表明存在能够解释这个问题的其他理论，但却没有一个完全可以确定的理论，也就是说motor theory of thinking不能完全被证明是正确的或是错误的，即选项(D)。

听力思路及考点总结

1. That is, if you put electrodes on the throat and measure muscle potential—muscle activity—you discover that when people are thinking, like if they're diligently trying to solve a problem, that there is muscular activity in the throat region.

   "That is"之后的内容要注意听，它是对前句话的解释，经常成为考点。

2. **Student**

   Professor Blake, um, did he happen to look at people who sign? I mean deaf people?

   Professor

   Uh, he did indeed, um, and to jump ahead, what one finds in deaf individuals who use sign language when they're given problems of various kinds, they have muscular changes in their hands when they are trying to solve a problem...muscle changes in the hand, just like the muscular changes going on in the throat region for speaking individuals.

   学生提问教授回答，或者是教授自问自答的这两种"问题—回答"模式经常成为考点。大家在听录音时，一定要注意位于这种位置的内容。

3. Ideomotor action is an activity that occurs without our noticing it, without our being aware of it. I'll give you one simple example.

   "Ideomotor action is..."这种表达通常是要下定义，而定义的出现是为了解释一个新的概念。考生若在听力考试时遇到下定义的句型，只需要知道新的概念大约表达了一个什么意思即可。但在本文中，"I'll give you one simple example"表示教授还要就这个概念举例，说明这个概念在文章中很重要。此时，考生就必须对这个概念所要表达的内容有清晰的记忆，它常常会成为考点。

4. Are there alternatives to this motor theory—this claim that muscular activities are equivalent to thinking? Is there anything else that might account for this change in muscular activity, other than saying that it is thinking? And the answer is clearly yes. Is there any way to answer the question definitively? I think the answer is no.

   这组句子很有代表性，经常在听力中出现。它所要表达的整体意思是"对某个问题目前还没有定论，还在讨论之中"。当考到对这类句子意思的理解时，直接选表达这个意思的选项即可。

Practice Set 4

讲座 ‖ 天文学·太阳系行星带的发现

题目解析

1

What is Bode's Law?

(A) A law of gravitation

(B) An estimate of the distance between Mars and Jupiter

(C) A prediction of how many asteroids there are

(D) A pattern in the spacing of the planets

Um, it isn't really a scientific law, not in the sense of predicting gravitation mathematically or something, **but it's attempting a pattern in the spacing of the planets**, and it was noticed by Bode hundreds of years ago. Well, you can imagine that there was some interest in why the 2.8 spot in the pattern was skipped, and um...but there wasn't anything obvious there, in the early telescopes. Then what happened in the late 1700s? The discovery of...?

注意听but之后的内容，往往是考点。本题中选项(D)与讲座内容完全一致。

注：本篇文章出题较乱，不符合正常的出题思路，没有太大参考价值。

2

Why does the professor explain Bode's Law to the class?

(A) To describe the size of the asteroids

(B) To explain how the asteroid belt was discovered

(C) To explain how gravitational forces influence the planets

(D) To describe the impact of telescopes on astronomy

Professor

OK. Let's get going. **Today I'm going to talk about how the asteroid belt was discovered**. And...I'm going to start by writing some numbers on the board. Here they are: We'll start with zero, then 3, ...6, ...12. Uh, tell me what I'm doing.

"Today I'm going to talk about" 之后的内容是这个讲座的主旨，常成为考点。在这个讲座中，教授先是列出了几组数字，目的是为了引出Bode's Law，而讲Bode's Law的目的又是为了解释asteroid belt是如何被人们发现的。故本题选项(B)为正确答案。

3

How does the professor introduce Bode's Law?

(A) By demonstrating how it is derived mathematically

(B) By describing the discovery of Uranus

(C) By drawing attention to the inaccuracy of a certain pattern

(D) By telling the names of several of the asteroids

We'll start with zero, then 3, ...6, ...12.

…

Right. I'm doubling the numbers, so 2 times 12 is 24, and the next one I'm going to write after 24 would be...

…

48. Then 96.

…

Professor

Right. In astronomical units—not perfect, but tantalizingly close. The value for Mars is off by...6 or 7 percent or so. It's...but it's within 10 percent of the average distance to Mars from the Sun. But I kind of have to skip the one after Mars for now. Then Jupiter's right there at 5-point something, and then Saturn is about 10 astronomical units from the Sun. **Um, well, this pattern is known as Bode's Law.**

在上题中刚刚解释过，教授列举几组数字的目的是为了介绍Bode's law，也就是通过数学演绎的方式引出Bode's law。故选项(A)正确。

4

Listen again to part of the lecture.

Then answer the question.

Why does the professor say this?

(A) To introduce an alternative application of Bode's Law

(B) To give an example of what Bode's Law cannot explain

(C) To describe the limitations of gravitational theory

(D) To contrast Bode's Law with a real scientific law

Um, well, this pattern is known as Bode's Law.

Um, it isn't really a scientific law, **not in the sense of predicting gravitation mathematically or something**, but it's attempting a pattern in the spacing of the planets, and it was noticed by Bode hundreds of years ago.

教授说这句话是为了表明Bode's Law不是scientific law。当讲"……不是……"时，是为了强调这两个事物之间的区别。注意在选项(D)中有contrast，与原文"...not..."相对应。contrast这个词用来比较两个事物之间的不同点，而compare这个词常用来比较两个事物之间的相同、相似之处。

5

According to the professor, what two factors contributed to the discovery of the asteroid Ceres?

Choose 2 answers.

(A) Improved telescopes

(B) Advances in mathematics

(C) The discovery of a new star

(D) The position of Uranus in a pattern

And look, **Uranus fits in the next spot in the pattern pretty nicely, um, not perfectly, but close**. And so then people got really excited about the validity of this thing and finding the missing object between Mars and Jupiter. **And telescopes, remember, were getting better**. So people went to work on finding objects that would be at that missing distance from the Sun, and then in 1801, the object Ceres was discovered.

本题只是对细节信息的考查，注意出题点位置的设置规律，见后面本文“听力思路及考点总结”的第四点。

6

What does the professor imply about the asteroid belt?

(A) It is farther from the Sun than Uranus.

(B) Bode believed it was made up of small stars.

(C) It is located where people expected to find a planet.

(D) Ceres is the only one of the asteroids that can be seen without a telescope.

Well, you can imagine that there was some interest in **why the 2.8 spot in the pattern was skipped, and um...but there wasn't anything obvious there, in the early telescopes**. Then what happened in the late 1700s? The discovery of...?

…

So people went to work on finding objects that would be at that missing distance from the Sun, and then in 1801, **the object Ceres was discovered**.

And Ceres was in the right place—the missing spot. Uh, but it was way too faint to be a planet. It looked like a little star. Uh, and because of its starlike appearance, um, it was called an "asteroid." OK? *Aster* is Greek for "star," as in *astronomy*. Um, and so, Ceres was the first and is the largest of what became many objects discovered at that same distance. Not just one thing, but all the objects found at that distance form the asteroid belt.

教授先提到2.8位置被跳过了，而在这个位置的前后都是planet，说明人们认为在2.8这个位置也应该存在一个planet。随后，他讲到了在1801年，人们在这个位置发现了Ceres。但Ceres太faint，不可以成为一个planet，就给它起名叫asteroid。后来又发现了很多这样的物质，形成了asteroid belt。这表明，在asteroid belt这个位置，人们曾经认为是应该有一颗planet的，即选项(C)正确。

听力思路及考点总结

1. Um, it isn't really a scientific law, not in the sense of predicting gravitation mathematically or something, but it's attempting a pattern in the spacing of the planets, and it was noticed by Bode hundreds of years ago.

   "It isn't..." 和 "...not" 部分的内容都没必要认真听，在这些有明确否定词出现的地方，一般不会是考点，但要注意听 "but..." 这部分肯定的内容。也就是说，否定性内容之后出现的肯定性内容往往会成为考点。

2. OK. Let’s get going. Today I’m going to talk about...

“Today I’m going to talk about”之后的内容要注意听，它往往是这堂课的主旨内容，常成为考点。

3. Then what happened in the late 1700s? The discovery of...?

Female student

Another planet?

Professor

The next planet out, Uranus—after Saturn.

“The discovery of...?”这句话表明教授在向学生提示“Then what happened in the late 1700s? ”这个问题的答案。这类考点经常在Listen Again题型中出现。

4. And telescopes, remember, were getting better.

“..., remember, ...”这个地方一定要注意听，它本身就是在强调所讲的这句话。含有remember的句子，往往会成为考点。

讲座‖植物学·植物纤维的用途

题目解析

1

What aspect of Manila hemp fibers does the professor mainly discribe in the lecture?

(A) ~~Similarities~~ between cotton fibers and Manila hemp fibers

(B) ~~Various types~~ of Manila hemp fibers

(C) The ~~economic importance~~ of Manila hemp fibers

(D) A use of Manila hemp fibers

本文先讲述了Manila hemp fibers的几个特征，接着解释它能在海上得到广泛应用的原因，最后又提到了如何把这种fiber做成绳子。只有选项(D)指明了讲座的主旨，即Manila hemp fibers的用途，故正确。

教授在开始的引言部分提到了cotton fibers，但并没有比较cotton fibers和Manila hemp fibers，没有比较就必然不会涉及两者的相似性(similarities)，故选项(A)错误。(B)、(C)两选项删除线部分未被原文提及，不予考虑。

听力技巧：教授说："上次课我们曾经讲过A……，这次课我们接着来讲B……"此时，注意听B部分的内容就可以了。A部分内容只为引出主题，一般不会成为考点。

2

Listen again to part of the lecture.

Then answer the question.

Why does the professor mention going away for the weekend?

(A) To tell the class a joke

(B) To apologize for not completing some work

(C) To introduce the topic of the lecture

(D) To encourage students to ask about her trip

Hi, everyone. Good to see you all today. Actually, I expected the population to be a lot lower today. It typically runs between 50 and 60 percent on the day the research paper is due. Um, I was hoping to have your exams back today, but, uh, the situation was that I went away for the weekend, and I was supposed to get in yesterday at five, and I expected to fully complete all the exams by midnight or so, which is the time that I usually go to bed, **but my flight was delayed**, and I ended up not getting in until one o'clock in the morning. Anyway, **I'll do my best to have them finished by the next time we meet.**

教授解释道由于航班晚点，她的工作没有按原计划完成，但保证会在下次上课之前把试卷评完。说这些话的目的是向学生们解释未评完试卷的原因，并向大家道歉。选项(B)正确。

如果题目这样问：教授为什么会说“OK. In the last class, we started talking about useful fibers. In particular, we talked about cotton fibers, which we said were very useful, not only in the textile industry, but also in the chemical industry, and in the production of many products, such as plastics, paper, explosives, and so on.”，那么选项(C)可以成为正确答案，因为提到这句话是为了引出本次课的主题。选项(A)“为了给学生讲个笑话”，以及选项(D)“为了鼓励学生提一些关于她旅行的问题”完全与本题无关。

3

What does the professor imply about the name "Manila hemp"?

(A) It is a ~~commercial brand name~~.

(B) Part of the name is inappropriate.

(C) The name has recently ~~changed~~.

(D) The name was ~~first used in the 1940s~~.

Now, for some strange reason, many people believe that Manila hemp is a hemp plant. **But Manila hemp is not really hemp.** It's actually a member of banana family—it even bears little banana-shaped fruits. **The "Manila" part of the name makes sense**, because Manila hemp is produced chiefly in the Philippine Islands and, of course, the capital city of the Philippines is Manila.

教授指出"Manila hemp"这个名称容易让人误解它是一种hemp，可它实际上是banana family的一个成员。而这个名称中的"Manila"部分是对的，因为它主要产于菲律宾，而菲律宾的首都是Manila。因此选项(B)正确，它指出了"Manila hemp"这个名称中的一部分（hemp）并不恰当。

4

Why does the professor mention the Golden Gate Bridge?

(A) To demonstrate a disadvantage of steel cables

(B) To give an example of the ~~creative use of color~~

(C) To show that steel cables ~~are able to~~ resist salt water

(D) To give an example of ~~a use of Manila hemp~~

Now, why was that? Well, **the main reason was that steel cables degrade very, very quickly in contact with salt water**. If you've ever been to San Francisco, you know that the Golden Gate Bridge is red. And it's red because of the zinc paint that goes on those stainless steel cables. That, if they start at one end of the bridge and they work to the other end, by the time they finish, it's already time to go back and start painting the beginning of the bridge again, because the bridge was built with steel cables, and steel cables can't take the salt air unless they're treated repeatedly with a zinc-based paint.

教授指出，尽管早在20世纪40年代steel cables就出现了，但大多数人仍然用Manila hemp ropes来泊船，原因是steel cables在含有盐分的海水里很容易被腐蚀。接着又用Golden Gate Bridge这个例子来说明steel cables容易被海水腐蚀这一事实。故选项(A)正确。

5

According to the professor, what was the main reason that many ships used Manila hemp ropes instead of steel cables?

(A) Manila hemp was cheaper.

(B) Manila hemp was easier to produce.

(C) Manila hemp is more resistant to salt water.

(D) Manila hemp is lighter in weight.

Now, as fibers go, Manila hemp fibers are very long. They can easily be several feet in length and they're also very strong, very flexible. They have one more characteristic that's **very important, and that is that they are exceptionally resistant to salt water.** And this combination of characteristics—long, strong, flexible, resistant to salt water—makes Manila hemp a great material for ropes, especially for ropes that are gonna be used on ocean-going ships. In fact, by the early 1940's, even though steel cables were available, most ships in the United States Navy were not moored with steel cables; they were moored with Manila hemp ropes.

本题正确答案为选项(C)。Manila hemp fibers的resistance to salt water这个特性被教授反复强调，这里在答案中出现，则必选。

听力技巧：若听力材料中反复提及的某个内容在某个选项中出现，则该选项往往是正确答案。

6

According to the lecture, what are two ways to increase the strength of rope made from Manila hemp fibers?

Choose 2 answers.

(A) Coat the fibers with zinc-based paint

(B) Combine the fibers into bundles

(C) Soak bundles of fibers in salt water

(D) Twist bundles of fibers

OK. So how do you take plant fibers that individually you could break with your hands and turn them into a rope that's strong enough to moor a ship that weighs thousands of tons? Well, what you do is you extract these long fibers from the Manila hemp plant, and then you take several of these fibers, and **you group them into a bundle**, because by grouping the fibers you greatly increase their breaking strength—that bundle of fibers is much stronger than any of the individual fibers that compose it. **And then you take that bundle of fibers and you twist it a little bit**, because by twisting it, you increase its breaking strength even more. And then you take several of these little bundles, and you group and **twist them into bigger bundles**, which you then group and **twist into even bigger bundles**, and so on, until eventually, you end up with a very, very strong rope.

本题只考查细节辨认能力。

听力思路及考点总结

1. In the last class, we talked about X... Today we'll continue talking about Y...

   Y为考点。

2. Now, for some strange reason, many people believe...

   这种表达暗示"大多数人认为的……"通常情况下都是错误的，不用认真听，但注意听它后面的正确观点，那才是真正的考点。

3. Now, as fibers go, Manila hemp fibers are very long...and they're also very strong, very flexible.

   注意听very long, very strong, very flexible这几个词，它们都被重读，并且读音也被延长。这些都是在强调该内容的重要性，常常成为考点。

4. They have one more characteristic that's very important, and that is that they are exceptionally resistant to salt water.

   在本句中，"one more..."说明教授在承接前文，并进一步补充一些内容。

   听到这种表达时要注意：

   (1) 前文的要点是什么；

   (2) 进一步补充的这个要点又是什么。

   这些内容往往成为考点。另外本句含有"...is very important"，考生必须注意，"..."这部分内容一定会成为最终的考点。

5. Now, why was that? Well, ...

   自问自答处，往往有考点出现，听出主要答案即可。

   此表达形式也出现在讲座最后一部分中：OK. So how do you take plant fibers that individually you could break with your hands and turn them into a rope that's strong enough to moor a ship that weighs thousands of tons? Well, ...

6. On the other hand, ...

   这个句型表达转折关系，注意听它后面的内容，该内容是说话者要强调的内容，通常会成为考点。

Conversation 1(Q1–Q5)

对话 ‖ 关于研究生入学申请的修改

题目解析

1

Why does the student go to see the professor?

(A) To prepare for her ~~graduate school interview~~

(B) To get advice about her graduate school application

(C) To ~~give~~ the professor her graduate school application

(D) To find out ~~if she was accepted into~~ graduate school

Professor

Hey, Ellen. How are you doing?

Student

Oh, pretty good, thanks. How are you?

Professor

OK.

Student

Did you, um, have a chance to look at my grad school application...you know, the statement of purpose I wrote.

Professor

Well, yeah. In fact, here it is. I just read it.

学生在这里一开始就问教授“您看了我研究生申请的个人陈述了吗？”由此可知，学生的主要目的是请教授给她一些关于这个陈述的意见。选项(B)正确。

grad school application = graduate school application

听力技巧：最前面打招呼／寒暄的内容不用听，需注意听后面疑问句的内容。位于对话最开始部分的疑问内容往往是对话的主旨，很有可能成为考点。

2

According to the professor, what information should the student include in her statement of purpose?

Choose 2 answers.

(A) Her academic motivation

(B) Her background ~~in medicine~~

(C) Some personal information

(D) The ways her ~~teachers have influenced her~~

Professor

So you might just break them out into, uh...you know, separate paragraphs and expand on each point some. But really what's critical with these is that, um, you've gotta **let yourself come through**. See, you gotta let them see you in these statements. Expand some more on what's happened in your own life and what shows your...**your motivation** and interest in this area—in geology. Let'em see what really, what... what captures your imagination about this field.

Student

OK. **So make it a little more...personal?** That's OK?

Professor

That's fine. **They look for that stuff**. You don't wanna go overboard...

Student

Right.

Professor

...but it's critical that...that somebody sees what your passion is—your personal motivation for doing this.

本题只是对细节信息的考查。

3

What does the professor consider unusual about the student's background?

(A) Her ~~work experience~~

~~(B)~~ Her ~~creative writing experience~~

~~(C)~~ Her ~~athletic achievements~~

(D) Her music training

Professor

And that's gotta come out in here. Um, and let's see, uh, you might also give a little, uh—since this is your only chance to do it, you might give a little more explanation about your unique undergraduate background. **So, you know, how you went through, you know, the music program;** what you got from that; why you decided to change. **I mean, it's kind of unusual to go from music to geology, right?**

教授在这里明确指出，学生由学习音乐转向学习地质学是一种比较特殊的情况。故本题正确答案为选项(D)。注意本题考点的设置，详细解释见后面关于本文的“听力思路及考点总结”。

4

Why does the professor tell a story about his friend who went to medical school?

(A) To warn the student about ~~how difficult~~ graduate school can be

(B) To illustrate a point he is making

(C) To help the student ~~relax~~

(D) To ~~change the subject~~

Professor

No, in fact it's...um, give an example: I...I had a friend, when I was an undergrad, um, went to medical school. And he put on his med school application—and he could actually tell if somebody actually read it 'cause, um, he had asthma and the reason that he wanted to go to med school was he said he wanted to do sports medicine because he, you know, he had this real interest. He was an athlete too, and...and wanted to help athletes who had this physical problem. And he could always tell if somebody actually read his letter because they would always ask him about that.

Student

...Mmm...so something unique.

Professor

Yeah. **So see, you know, that's what's good and, and, I think for you probably, you know, your music background's the most unique thing that you've got in your record.**

教授的主要建议之一就是让学生将陈述写得更加有个性一些，能够表现出自己与众不同的地方。而这个例子正是为了说明这一点，故选项(B)是正确答案。

5

What does the professor imply about the people who admit students to graduate school?

(A) They often ~~lack expertise~~ in the fields of the applicants.

(B) They ~~do not usually read~~ the statement of purpose.

(C) They are influenced by the appearance of an application.

(D) They ~~remember most of the applications~~ they receive.

Professor

Also, think about presentation—how the application looks. In a way you're actually showing some other skills here, like organization. A lot of stuff that's...that they're not...they're not formally asking for, they're looking at. So your presentation format, your grammar, all that stuff, they're looking at in your materials at the same time.

教授在这里建议学生要注意陈述的形式，如格式、语法等，并且指明这些虽然不是招生委员会明确要求的，但却是他们在读这些申请陈述时会注意到的。故本题答案为选项(C)。

听力思路及考点总结

1. Did you, um, have a chance to look at my grad school application...you know, the statement of purpose I wrote.

   "...um, ..." "...you know, ..." 这样的表达表示说话的延迟（通常其后会出现请求性的内容）或强调其后的内容，这些地方常成为听力的考点。与此类似的表达还有："...you know what, ..." "...guess what..."

2. But really what's critical with these is that, um, you've gotta let yourself come through.

   "what's critical" 后的内容经常是听力中的考点，因为这种句型的语义本身就是强调它后面的内容是重要的。

3. Um, and let's see, uh, you might also give a little, uh—since this is your only chance to do it, you might give a little more explanation about your unique undergraduate background.

   "You might also..." 是建议句型，往往成为考点。其具体内容可见Practice Set 1后面的"听力思路与考点总结"。

4. I mean it's kind of unusual to go from music to geology, right?

   "I mean..." 这种表达用来解释前文内容，常成为考点。且本句为反问句，表达一种肯定的态度，这也是在听力考试中需要注意的地方。

5. Yeah. So see, you know, that's what's good and, and, I think for you probably, you know, your music background's the most unique thing that you've got in your record.

   这句话中包含一个最高级"the most unique thing..."，最高级是一种比较特殊的语言现象，在听力中出现时，一定要注意，它往往会成为考点。

Conversation 2(Q6–Q10)

对话 || 关于生物考试前的复习

题目解析

6

What are the students mainly discussing?

(A) ~~Drugs~~ that are harmful to the human body

(B) Bacteria that ~~produce~~ antibiotics

(C) ~~DNA~~ that is related to athletic performance

(D) Genes that protect bacteria from antibiotics

Male student

OK, so...what do you think we should go over next?

Female student

How about if **we go over this stuff about how bacteria become resistant to antibiotics**.

Male student

OK.

…

Male student

About how bacteria become resistant to antibiotics.

男生先用提问的方式（what do you think we should...）引出对话内容的主题，女生继而用建议的方式（how about if we...）表明对话的主题。做本题时，考生应该注意建议句型作为考点的情况。

7

Listen again to part of the conversation. Then answer the question.

Why does the woman say this?

(A) To find out if the man has done his assignment

(B) To ask the man to find out if the library is open

(C) To let the man know that she cannot study much longer

(D) To ask if the man has ever met her roommate

Female student

Um, but first of all, though, how many pages do we have left? I told my roommate I'd meet her at the library at seven o'clock.

女生说："现在我们还剩几页没有看？我和我室友约好了，七点和她在图书馆见面。"这句话表明她不会和这个男生讨论得太久，因为等会儿还有其他事情要做。故本题正确答案为选项(C)。

8

According to the conversation, why are transposons sometimes called "jumping genes"?

(A) They are able to move from one bacteria cell to another.

(B) They are found in people with exceptional jumping ability.

(C) They occur in every other generation of bacteria.

(D) Their movements are rapid and unpredictable.

Male student

Lemme see. OK. Trans...po...sons...trans...posons. So "transposon" is another name for a jumping gene?

Female student

Right. And these transposons are, **you know, like, little bits of DNA that are able to move from one cell to another**. That's why they're called "jumping genes." They kind of, you know, **"jump" from one cell to another**.

本题考点是对新概念的解释。请注意，该考点在对话中以重复的形式被着重指出。

9

According to the conversation, what are two ways in which bacteria cells get resistance genes?

Choose 2 answers.

(A) The resistance genes are carried from nearby cells.

(B) The resistance genes are carried by white blood cells.

(C) The resistance genes are inherited from the parent cell.

(D) The resistance genes are carried by antibiotics.

Female student

OK. But the question is: how do bacteria get the resistance genes?

Male student

How do they get the resistance genes? **They just inherit them from the parent cell, right?**

Female student

OK, yeah, that's true. **They can inherit them from the parent cell**, but that's not what I'm talking about.

Male student

OK.

Female student

I'm talking about **how they get resistance genes from other cells in their environment, you know, from the other cells around them**.

Male student

Oh, I see what you mean. Umm, is that that stuff about "hopping genes," or something like that?

Female student

Right. Although actually they're called "jumping genes" not "hopping genes."

Male student

Oh, OK. Jumping genes.

本题是对细节信息的考查，请注意对话中信息的不断重复和考点的设置。

10

What can be inferred about the resistance genes discussed in the conversation?

(A) They are found in all bacteria cells.

(B) They are not able to resist antibiotics.

(C) They make the treatment of bacterial diseases more difficult

(D) They are essential to the body's defenses against bacteria.

Female student

Oh yeah, OK. So you know that **some bacteria cells are able to resist the drugs we use against them, and that's because they have these special genes that, like, protect them from the drugs**.

Male student

Right. If I remember correctly, I think the genes like...**weaken the antibiotics, or, like...stop the antibiotics from getting into the bacteria cell**, something like that?

...

Male student

That's how **it becomes resistant to antibiotics**.

对话中这几处都表明resistance genes能够削弱antibiotics（抗生素）的功能，使细胞对药物产生抗体，也就是说这些resistance genes的存在会使治疗疾病更加困难。故选项(C)正确。

听力思路及考点总结

1. What do you think we should go over next?

   这句话是典型的引起下文的说法，要注意听对这个问题的回答，答案经常成为考点。

2. How about if we go over this stuff about how bacteria become resistant to antibiotics.

   "How about if..."是建议句型，其后面的内容常为考点。

3. And these transposons are, you know, like, little bits of DNA that are able to move from one cell to another.

   ★ "you know..."之后的内容容易成为考点。

   ★ 本句话中含有比较句式：like...。听力中，若含有比较句式，则需注意听比较的对象和内容分别是什么，经常是考点所在。

   常考的比较句式还有以下几种：

   unlike A..., B...

   similar to A..., B...

   A is differed from B, which...

   (just) as A..., B...

4. Um, but first of all, though, how many pages do we have left? I told my roommate I'd meet her at the library at seven o'clock.

   这种句子的含义经常作为考点，它所表达的意思是说话者有其他事情要做，不能聊太久。

5. How do they get the resistance genes? They just inherit them from the parent cell, right?

   此句是设问句，容易成为考点。同时，后半句话还用了反义疑问句，反义疑问句在听力中起加强语气的作用，用疑问的形式表示肯定，这样的句子也容易成为考点。

Lecture 1(Q11–Q16)

讲座 || 环境科学 • 地下水资源的利用

题目解析

11

What is the talk mainly about?

(A) A common method of managing water supplies

(B) The ~~formation~~ of underground water systems

(C) ~~Natural processes~~ that renew water supplies

(D) Maintaining the ~~purity~~ of underground water systems

Professor

So I wanted to discuss a few other terms here...actually, some, uh, **some ideas about how we manage our resources**. Let's talk about what that...what that means. If we take a resource like water... well, maybe we should get a little bit more specific here—back up from the more general case—and talk about underground water in particular.

...

Wrong, but that's the principle. That's the idea behind how we manage our water supplies. **It's called "safe yield."** Basically what this method says is that you can pump as much water out of a system as naturally recharges...as naturally flows back in.

教授在讲座开头就用句型（I wanted to discuss...）指出了本文的主旨内容。故本题正确选项为(A)。

12

What is the professor's point of view concerning the method of "safe yield"?

(A) It has helped to preserve the environment.

(B) It should be researched in states other than Arizona.

(C) It is not an effective resource policy.

(D) It ignores the different ways people use water.

本题较难，无法根据原文中具体的一句话或几句话推测出本题的答案。教授在讲座过程中一直对safe yield这种方法持负评价。这种方法只考虑到了人为因素（人类可以抽取地下水），但忽略了自然因素（自然界中的水也是通过地下水来补给的）。一旦人类取水过多，自然界中的水将无法得到充足的补给。因此这并不是一种管理地下水的好方法，故本题正确答案为选项(C)。

13

According to the professor, what are two problems associated with removing water from an underground system?

Choose 2 answers.

(A) Pollutants can enter the water more quickly.

(B) The surface area can dry and crack.

Professor

Right. We take water out, but water also naturally flows out. And the recharge rate doesn't change, so the result is we've reduced the amount of water that's stored in the underground system.

If you keep doing that long enough—if you pump as much water out as naturally

(C) The amount of water stored in the system can drop.

(D) Dependent streams and springs can dry up.

comes in—**gradually the underground water levels drop**. And when that happens, that can affect surface water. How? Well, in underground systems there are natural discharge points—places where the water flows out of the underground systems, out to lakes and streams. Well, a drop in the water level can mean those discharge points will eventually dry up. That means **water's not getting to lakes and streams that depend on it. So we've ended up reducing the surface water supply, too.**

本题是对细节信息的考查。

14

Listen again to part of the lecture.

Then answer the question.

Why does the professor say this?

(A) To find out whether the students are familiar with the issue

(B) To introduce a new problem for discussion

(C) To respond to a student's question

(D) To encourage the students to care about the topic.

Now, why is this an issue? Well, aren't some of you going to want to live in this state for a while? Want your kids to grow up here, and your kids' kids?

这句话可翻译为“这为什么会成为一个问题？难道你们不打算在这儿居住下去吗？不想让你们的孩子以及孩子的孩子在这里长大吗？”教授说这句话是为了启发学生们从更长远的角度来思考前面讲到的问题。故本题正确答案为选项(D)。

15

What is a key feature of a sustainable water system?

(A) It is able to satisfy short-term and long-term needs.

(B) It is not affected by changing environmental conditions.

(C) It usually originates in lakes, springs, or streams.

(D) It is not used to supply human needs.

Now, why is this an issue? Well, aren't some of you going to want to live in this state for a while? Want your kids to grow up here, and your kids' kids? You might be concerned with…does Arizona have a water supply which is sustainable—**key word here? What that means...the general definition of *sustainable* is will there be enough to meet the needs of the present without compromising the ability of the future to have the availability...to have the same resources?**

本题考的是一种同义替代，原文中的present与答案中的short-term所表达的意思相同，原文中的future与答案中的long-term所表达的意思相同。故正确答案为选项(A)。

16

What does the professor imply about water systems managed by the "safe-yield" method?

(A) They recharge at a rapid rate.

(B) They are not sustainable.

(C) They must have large storage areas.

(D) They provide a poor quality of water.

Now, I hope you see that these two ideas are **incompatible: sustainability and safe yield**. Because what sustainability means is that it's sustainable for all systems dependent on the water—for the people that use it and for...uh, for supplying water to the dependent lakes and streams.

So I'm gonna repeat this: so, if we're using a safe-yield method, if we're only balancing what we take out with what gets recharged, but—don't forget, water's also flowing out naturally—then the amount stored underground is gonna gradually get reduced and that's gonna lead to another problem. These discharge points—where the water flows out to the lakes and streams—they're gonna dry up. OK.

教授指出sustainability和safe yield这两者是互不相容的（incompatible）。因此可以推断出safe yield方法并不具备可持续性（not sustainable）。故本题正确答案是选项(B)。

听力思路及考点总结

1. So I wanted to discuss a few other terms here...actually, some, uh, some ideas about how we manage our resources.

   "I wanted to discuss..." 这种开头句型往往是要引出文章的主题。

2. So hydrogeologists have tried to figure out...how much water can you take out from underground sources? This has been an important question.

   "...an important question" 这句话要注意听，显然这里要说一个重要的问题。

3. Let me ask you guys: how much water, based on what you know so far, could you take out of, say, an aquifer...under the city?

   这种句型通常会成为考点。注意对这个问题的回答，这往往是某个问题的正确答案所在。

4. You might be concerned with...does Arizona have a water supply which is sustainable—key word here? What that means...the general definition of sustainable is will there be enough to meet the needs of the present without compromising the ability of the future to have the availability...to have the same resources?

"key word" 强调 "sustainable" 这个词是重要的。在听力过程中，应该注意听教授对这个新名词的解释。

5. I'm gonna repeat this: so, if we're using a safe-yield method, if we're only balancing what we take out with what gets recharged, but—don't forget, water's also flowing out naturally—then the amount stored underground is gonna gradually get reduced and that's gonna lead to another problem.

"I'm gonna repeat this" 之后的内容要注意听，是教授要强调的内容，常常成为考点。

Lecture 2(Q17–Q22)

讲座 || 哲学 · 柏拉图的道德理论

题目解析

17

Why does the professor talk about Plato's description of society?

(A) To explain why ~~societies face certain problems~~

(B) To point out ~~problems with Plato's ethical theory~~

(C) To introduce students to ~~the political structure of ancient Greece~~

(D) To help explain Plato's view about the nature of the human soul

教授先讲Plato认为的构成良好社会的三个要素，之后又指出Plato认为构成品质良好的个人的要素与构成社会的三个要素相似。因此，教授对社会要素进行描述是为了解释Plato对于个人本质的观点。故本题正确答案为选项(D)。

18

Listen again to part of the lecture. Then answer the question.

What does the professor imply about Plato's ethical theory?

Now, some of you may have studied Plato's philosophy in some other course, so this might be easy. OK. At the risk of boring you, let me give you just an overview of Plato's ethical theory.

(A) It may be familiar to some of the students.

(B) It will be discussed in more detail in a later class.

(C) It is not an interesting theory.

(D) It is not a very complicated theory.

这几句话可翻译为“你们中的一些可能在其他的课程中学过Plato的哲学，现在接受起来会容易一些。不过大家可能会觉得无趣，（因为会和大家以前学过的内容有些重复，）我就大致介绍一下Plato关于道德方面的理论。”这句话表明一些学生可能学过这个方面的内容，对于这个话题并不陌生。故本题正确答案为选项(A)。

19

Listen again to part of the lecture. Then answer the question.

Why does the professor ask this?

(A) To find out if students have understood what she just said

(B) To suggest an answer to a question that she just asked

(C) To express disagreement with a point made by Plato

(D) To explain why harmony is difficult for a society to achieve

But why? Why do workers and soldiers have to learn self-control? **Well, how can a society flourish if the workers and soldiers don't control their desires and emotions?**

这几句话可翻译为“但是为什么呢？为什么工人和士兵要学会自制？如果工人和士兵不能控制他们的欲望和情绪，一个社会又如何能繁荣呢？”教授说最后一个反义疑问句是为了提示这个问题的答案，为学生指出回答这个问题的方向。可见，选项(B)是正确答案。

听力技巧：这里，教授在提出一个问题后又补充了一些内容。这种补充性的内容往往是对如何回答这个问题作提示，而这种提示性作用经常成为考点。

20

What are two points that reflect Plato's views about education?

Choose 2 answers.

(A) All people can be trained to become leaders.

(B) All people should learn to use their intellect.

(C) Leaders should be responsible for the education of workers and soldiers.

(D) All people should learn about the nature of the human soul.

But you're not going to get that automatically. You need to teach them this kind of moderation. So you need an educational system that **first of all will train the leaders, so that they'll make good decisions, so they'll know what's wise**. Then **make leaders responsible—um, uh, turn over to them the education of the other two groups**. And through education, build a society **so that the workers and soldiers learn to use their intellect to control their desires and emotions**. If you had all that, then, for Plato, you'd have a good or just society.

本题是对细节信息的考查。

21

Based on information in the lecture, indicate whether the statements below about human emotion reflect beliefs held by Plato.

Well, these soldiers, well, they're going to be in dangerous situations quite frequently, so you need people with, um, a...a lot of high spirit—uh, an emotional type of

Emotion is usually controlled by the faculty of desire. (**NO**)

Emotion ought to be controlled by the faculty of intellect. (**YES**)

Emotion is what motivates soldiers. (**YES**)

individual. **Emotion is what characterizes this group.**

…

In each of us, our desires and emotions often get the better of us, and lead us to do foolish things. They're in conflict with the intellect. So, to get them to all work together, to coexist in harmony, every person needs to be shaped in the same way that we've shaped society—through the educational system. **Individuals must be educated to use their intellect to control their emotions and desires.** That's harmony in the soul.

根据讲座原文，emotion是被intellect控制的，并不是desire。即第一个选项错误。

22

According to Plato, what is the main characteristic of a good or just person?

(A) The parts of the person's soul exist in harmony.

(B) The person does not try to control other people.

(C) The person's relationships with other people are harmonious.

(D) The person does not act in an emotional manner.

Now, take that picture—that social, political picture—and apply it to the individual person. You remember about the soul? That it consists of three separate parts, or faculties? Can you guess what they are? Desires, emotions, and intellect—the characteristics associated with the three groups of society. And can you guess how Plato defines a good or just person? Well, **it's parallel to how he characterizes a good or just society. The three have to be in harmony.**

注意本题的考点在设问位置，即教授的自问自答。另外，该题也含有关于比较的考点：it's parallel to...，这个表达表示两个事物之间的共同点。

听力思路及考点总结

1. So we'll start with Plato—Plato's philosophy.

   "we'll start with..." 这种开头句型经常用于引出文章的主题。

2. He believed that goodness in an individual was to be found when the three parts of the soul worked together, when they weren't in conflict, but existed in harmony. A good or just person will have a soul in which the three faculties work well together.

   "...when they weren't..., but..." 前部分否定，后部分肯定，肯定部分容易成为考点。另外，"A good or just person will have a soul in which the three faculties work well together" 的意思是对 "but existed in harmony" 意思的重复，这种意思重复的地方也容易成为考点。

3. He argues that every society has to have three groups of people: workers, soldiers, and leaders. And each has a sort of defining characteristic.

   这句话是表示分类的句子，它表明随后教授会分别陈述每个类别的特征。

4. And can you guess how Plato defines a good or just person? Well, it's parallel to how he characterizes a good or just society.

   注意本句是设问和比较两个考点的结合。

Lecture 3(Q23–Q28)

讲座 || 植物学 • 植物的根系生长

题目解析

23

What is the main topic of the lecture?

(A) The size of root systems

(B) ~~Various types~~ of root systems

(C) The ~~nutrients~~ required by rye plants

(D) ~~Improving~~ two types of plant species

Professor

OK. So we've talked about some different types of root systems of plants, and I've shown you some pretty cool slides, **but now I want to talk about the extent of the root system—the overall size of the root system...the depth**. I want to tell you about one particular experiment. I think you're going to find this pretty amazing. OK. So there was this scientist...this very meticulous scientist decided that the best place to see a whole root system—to actually see how big the entire system got—the best place would be to grow it...where?

此类考点在前文中已经被提及。当教授说"本次课我们要讲……"时，这部分内容通常是本文的主旨内容。

24

According to the professor, why did one scientist grow a rye plant in water?

(A) To expose the roots to ~~sunlight~~

(B) To be able to ~~fertilize it with gas~~

(C) To be able to see its entire root system

(D) To see ~~how minerals penetrate~~ its roots

Professor

...OK. So there was this scientist...this very meticulous scientist decided that **the best place to see a whole root system—to actually see how big the entire system got—the best place would be to grow it... where?**

Female student

Um, **water**?

Professor

In water. So he took rye plants—it was rye plants—and he started growing them in water...

...

Professor

Respire...respiration...they breathe. So, if you just stick rye plants in water, it doesn't make a difference how much fertilizer you add, you also need to bubble gas through the water, so they have access to that oxygen. If they don't have that, they're in big trouble. **OK. So this guy—this scientist—grew a rye plant in water so he could see the root system, how big it got—its surface area.**

本题涉及三个考点：

(1) 最高级出现的位置：the best place

(2) 疑问句出现的位置：the best place would be to grow it...where?

(3) 对上文意思的重复：So this guy—this scientist—grew a rye plant in water so he could see the root system, how big it got—its surface area.

25

Listen again to part of the lecture.

Then answer the question.

Why did the professor say this?

(A) She wanted to correct the wording of a previous statement.

(B) She wishes she did not have to bubble gas through it.

(C) She realized the odor of gas could be unpleasant.

(D) She forgot to tell the students about a step in the experiment.

What do you need to do to that water besides put fertilizer in it? Anyone ever actually tried to grow plants in water? You must bubble water through it. Bubble gas through it. **I'm sorry, you must bubble gas through it.** So, gas, you have to bubble through.

教授开始说要向水里再注入水(bubble water)，接着意识到自己说错了，然后改正说应该向水里注入空气(bubble gas)。所以教授说 "I'm sorry, you must bubble gas through it" 的目的是更正刚刚的口误。选项(A)是正确答案。

26

The professor mentions houseplants that receive too much water. Why does she mention them?

Professor

Right. They grow all kinds of commercial crops in water. So, if you're growing things

(A) To show that ~~many different types~~ of plants can grow in water

(B) To explain why plants grown in water should have a gas bubbled through them

(C) To remind the students of the ~~importance of their next experiment~~

(D) To make a point about the ~~length of houseplants' roots~~

in water, you can add the fertilizer. What do you need to do to that water besides put fertilizer in it? Anyone ever actually tried to grow plants in water? You must bubble water through it. **Bubble gas through it. I'm sorry, you must bubble gas through it. So, gas, you have to bubble through.** Think about the soil we talked about last week, about growing plants in soil. Think about some of you who have killed your favorite houseplants, 'cause you loved them too much. If you overwater, why do your favorite houseplants die?

Female student

Oh, no oxygen.

Professor

Not enough oxygen for the roots...which do what twenty-four hours a day in all seasons?

Female student

Respiration?

Professor

Respire...respiration...they breathe. So, if you just stick rye plants in water, it doesn't make a difference how much fertilizer you add, **you also need to bubble gas through the water, so they have access to that oxygen.** If they don't have that, they're in big trouble.

听力中如果有例子出现，则要明确例子所说明的问题是什么。本题中，一个例子就成为了考点。另外，本题考点还涉及内容的重复。重复的内容就是说话者要强调的信息，而强调的信息自然是文章的重点内容，往往成为考点。

27

Listen again to part of the lecture.

Then answer the question.

What does the professor intend to explain?

(A) Why a mistake made in textbooks was never corrected

(B) Why she does not believe that the roots of rye plants extend to 1,000 kilometers

(C) How the roots of rye plants develop to such a great length

(D) How plants grown in water make use of fertilizer

I read about this and the book said one thousand kilometers of roots. I kept thinking: this has to be a mistake. It just doesn't make any sense to me that...that...that could be right. But that's what all the books have, and no one's ever corrected it. So **let me explain to you about this rye plant.**

教授说她读过一本书，里面介绍某种植物的根可以长到1000千米长，虽然她刚开始不敢相信，但这个信息确实是真的。接着她便要解释为什么这种植物的根可以长到那么长。故本题正确答案为选项(C)。

28

According to the professor, what similarity is there between crabgrass and rye plants?

(A) Both start growing in the month of May.

(B) Both have root systems that require a lot of water.

Professor

Crabgrass.

Remember how I showed you in the lab, **one little seed starts out producing one little shoot**. Then at a week or so later

(C) Both have more shoot surface than root surface.

(D) Both produce many shoots from a single seed.

you've got about six shoots, and then, three weeks later you've got about fifteen shoots coming out all directions like this—all those little shoots up there? Well, that's what they did with the rye. **And the little seedling started and pretty soon there were several shoots, and then more shoots**. In the end, that one single seed produced eighty shoots, with an average of fifty centimeters of height...from one seed. Eighty shoots coming out, average fifty centimeters high. When they looked at the shoot versus the root surface, they found that the shoot surface, with all of its leaves, had a total surface area of about five square meters. Now, here's the biggie: when they looked at the root surface area, you would expect that the root and the shoot would be in balance, right? So, they should be pretty close in terms of surface area, right?

教授先以crabgrass为例，讲它是如何从one seed长出many shoots的。接着指出rye plants也是这样的，之后又具体讲了rye plants如何从one seed长出eighty shoots的。故本题正确答案为选项(D)。

听力思路及考点总结

1. OK. So we've talked about some different types of root systems of plants, and I've shown you some pretty cool slides, but now I want to talk about the extent of the root system—the overall size of the root system...the depth.

   "...but now I want to talk about..." 这种开头句型经常用来引出文章的主题。

2. The best place would be to grow it...where?

   Female student

   Um, water?

   Professor

   In water. So he took rye plants—it was rye plants—and he started growing them in water. Now, you've all heard of growing stuff in water before, right?

   教授说"in water"，表示这个女生的回答是正确的。这种暗示性信息有时会成为Listen Again题型的考点。

3. **Professor**

   Not enough oxygen for the roots...which do what twenty-four hours a day in all seasons?

   Female student

   Respiration?

   Professor

   Respire...respiration...they breathe.

   教授说的"respire...respiration...they breathe"与考点2"in water"所表达的意义和意图相同。

4. Remember how I showed you in the lab, one little seed starts out producing one little shoot.

   在听这句话的时候，要格外注意，它含有"remember..."这个词，这样的句子常常成为考点。

5. Root hairs, that's exactly it. So those root hairs were responsible for an incredible chunk of surface area.

   后句话是对前句话意思的重复，容易成为考点。

Lecture 4(Q29-Q34)

讲座 || 商学 • 公司的两种组织架构

题目解析

29

What is the lecture mainly about?

(A) Technological innovations in the automobile industry

(B) The organizational structure of companies

(C) Ways to improve efficiency in an engineering department

(D) Methods of resolving conflicts in organizations

Professor

OK. Uh, **let's talk about organization and structure in a company.** How are companies typically structured?

Female student

Functionally.

教授用开头句式（let's talk about...）指明本次课程的主题：the organization and structure in a company。故本题正确答案为选项(B)。

30

Why does the professor talk about a construction company that has work in different cities?

(A) To give an example of functional organization

(B) To give an example of organization around projects

Female student

By projects.

Professor

Right. By function...and by projects. Twenty years ago companies were organized in function groups, where people with a certain expertise worked together as a unit—the, uh, architects in one unit, the finance people in another unit. **Well, nowadays a lot of companies are organized around projects**—like a

(C) To illustrate problems with functional organization

(D) To illustrate the types of conflict that can arise in companies

construction company could be building an office building in one city and an apartment house somewhere else, and each project has its own architects and engineers.

Now, the good thing about project organization is that it's easier to change to adapt to the needs of the project—it's a small group, a dedicated team, not the whole company.

教授先讲20年前很多公司都是organized in function groups，但现在很多公司都是organized around projects。后面又用construction company来举例说明organized around projects这类公司架构。故本题正确答案为选项(B)。

31

Listen again to part of the lecture.

Then answer the question.

Why does the professor say this?

(A) He does not understand why the student is talking about engineers.

(B) He wants to know how the engineers will communicate with their coworkers.

(C) The student has not provided a complete answer to his question.

(D) He wants the student to do more research on the topic.

Professor

Well...well, we'll appoint a manager: new car number one manager, car number two manager—they're completely responsible. Why should we have a single engineering department that has all four cars passing through it?

Female student

When you design a car, you need the expertise of all the engineers in the company. Each engineer needs to be in touch with the entire engineering department.

Professor

Yeah, but I keep...I keep asking why. I wanna know why. Yes.

尽管这位女生似乎已经回答了教授的提问，但教授仍一再问“为什么”。这表明学生的回答并不完整，没有涉及问题的本质。故本题正确答案为选项(C)。

32

What is an example of a violation of the “unity of command” principle?

(A) More than one person supervises the same employee.

(B) A company decides not to standardize its products.

(C) Several project managers are responsible for designing a new product.

(D) An employee does not follow a supervisor’s instructions.

Female student

Unity of command.

Professor

Unity of command. That’s exactly right. So this...this is a vicious violation of unity of command, isn’t it? **It says that this engineer working on a project seems to have two bosses.** We...we got the engineering boss, and we got the project manager boss. But the project manager is responsible for the project, and is not the official manager of the engineer who works on the project. And we try to maintain peace in the organizations, and sometimes it’s disrupted and we have conflicts, don’t we? The project manager for car one wants a car part to fit in a particular way, for a specific situation, a specialized case. Well, the, uh, engineering director says no, we gotta have standardization. We gotta have all the cars done this way. We can't make a special mold for that particular part for that particular car. We’re not gonna do that. So we got a conflict.

教授指明“这个工程师似乎有两个老板（this engineer working on a project seems to have two bosses）”的事实与“统一指挥（unity of command）”这个理念相冲突。故选项(A)正确。

33

According to the professor, where might there be a conflict in an organizational structure based on both projects and function?

(A) Between architects and finance experts

(B) Between the need to specialize and the need to standardize

(C) Between two engineers who work on the same project

(D) Between the needs of projects in different cities

Female student

Unity of command.

Professor

Unity of command. That's exactly right. So this...this is vicious violation of unity of command, isn't it? It says that this engineer working on a project seems to have two bosses.

We...we got the engineering boss, and we got the project manager boss. But the project manager is responsible for the project, and is not the official manager of the engineer who works on the project. And we try to maintain peace in the organizations and sometimes it's disrupted and **we have conflicts, don't we? The project manager for car one wants a car part to fit in a particular way, for a specific situation, a specialized case. Well, the, uh, engineering director says no, we gotta have standardization.** We gotta have all the cars done this way. We can't make a special mold for that particular part for that particular car. We're not gonna do that. So we got a conflict.

教授指出project manager对产品的specialized case负责，而engineerring director对产品的standardization负责。这就是功能性架构和项目性架构之间的冲突。故选项(B)正确。

34

Indicate whether each sentence below describes functional organization or project organization. Place a check mark in the correct box.

It encourages people with similar expertise to work closely together.
(**Functional Organization**)

It helps the company to adapt quickly and meet changing needs.
(**Project Organization**)

It helps to achieve uniformity in projects.
(**Functional Organization**)

本题是对细节信息的考查。

Now, the good thing about **project organization is that it's easier to change to adapt to the needs of the project**—it's a small group, a dedicated team, not the whole company.

...

Male student

Well, to eliminate redundancy's probably one of the biggest factors in an organization. So that, uh...so that there's **there's...standards of...for uniformity and efficiency in the organization.**

Professor

OK. And...and **that's probably the primary reason for functional organization** right there—is that we want some engineering consistency. We want the same kind of technology used in all four cars. If we disperse those four engineers into four parts of the organization and they work by themselves, there's a lot less chance that the technology's gonna be the same from car to car. So instead we maintain the functional organization—**that means the engineers work together in one part of the building.** And their offices are next to each other because we want them to talk to each other. When an engineer works on a project, they bring the expertise of their whole functional group with them.

听力思路及考点总结

1. OK. Uh, let’s talk about organization and structure in a company. How are companies typically structured?

“OK. Uh, let’s talk about...”这种开头句型用来引出文章的主题。

2. Now, the good thing about project organization is that it’s easier to change to adapt to the needs of the project—it's a small group, a dedicated team, not the whole company.

“the good thing about...is...”这种句型用于陈述某个事物的优点，而这个优点经常成为考点。

3. ...here’s a question for you: Why do we continue to organize ourselves by function, even now, when in fact we admit that projects are the lifeblood of a lot of organizations? Why do some companies maintain a functional organization instead of organizing around projects?

“here’s a question for you...”表明这个问题非常重要，因此一定要听清楚这个问题的正确答案是什么。

4. Well, to eliminate redundancy’s probably one of the biggest factors in an organization. So that, uh...so that there’s, there’s...standards of...for uniformity and efficiency in the organization.

这句话含有最高级（the biggest factors...），在听的时候要多加注意。

5. And...and that’s probably the primary reason for functional organization right there—is that we want some engineering consistency.

“primary reason”强调此处提到的这个原因是非常重要的。听的时候要多加注意。

Authentic TOEFL Practice Test 2

Conversation 1(Q1–Q5)

对话 || 讨论商业心理学课的一个作业

题目解析

1

Why does the student go to see the professor?

(A) For suggestions on how to write interview questions

(B) For assistance in finding a person to interview

(C) To ask for advice on starting a business

(D) To schedule an interview with him

2

Why does the student mention her high school newspaper?

(A) To inform the professor that she plans to print the interview there

(B) To explain why the assignment is difficult for her

(C) To show that she enjoys writing for school newspapers

(D) To indicate that she has experience with conducting interviews

Professor

Are you having trouble coming up with interview questions?

Female Student

Well, that's just it. **I mean I worked on my high school newspaper for years, so I actually have great questions to ask.** The thing is…I'm new to the area, and I don't know people off campus…**So, I was wondering if…well, could you possibly give me the name of someone I could interview…?**

3

How does the professor help the student?

(A) He gives her a list of local business owners.

(B) He allows her to interview business owners in her hometown.

(C) He suggests that she read the business section of the newspaper.

(D) He gives her more time to complete the assignment.

Professor

Well, it wouldn't be fair to the other students if I gave you the name of a contact—but I could help you figure out a way to find someone on your own. Let's see...**Do you read the local newspaper?**

Female Student

Sure, whenever I have the time.

Professor

Well, **the business section** in the paper often has stories about local business people who've been successful. If you find an article, you could call the person who is profiled.

注意：因为听力部分的考点在前面的题目讲解过程中已经全部涵盖，Authentic TOEFL Practice Test 2＆3中的题目基本上是对前面各种考点的不断重复，所以一些简单的、可以由原文信息直接对应答案的题，就只标明关系。只有一些稍有难度的题，才在后面给出具体的解析。另外，在每篇文章后也不再列“听力思路及考点总结”，因为重要考点前面差不多都提到了。请考生在看这两套题时，主动思考，多联系前面讲过的内容，举一反三，真正地理解那些重点解题思路。

4

What does the professor want the students to learn from the assignment?

(A) That starting a business is risky

(B) Why writing articles on local businesses is important

(C) How to develop a detailed business plan

(D) What personality traits are typical of business owners

Professor

Many people enjoy telling the story of how they got started. **Remember**, this is a business psychology class, and for this assignment, **I want you to get some real insight about business owners, their personality, what drives them to become an entrepreneur.**

Female Student

Like, how they think?

Professor

And what motivates them. Why did they start their business?

5

Listen again to part of the conversation. Then answer the question.

What does the student imply?

(A) She is surprised by the professor's reaction.

(B) The professor has not quite identified her concern.

(C) The professor has guessed correctly what her problem is.

(D) She does not want to finish the assignment.

Professor

Are you having trouble coming up with interview questions?

Female Student

Well, that's just it. I mean, I worked on my high school newspaper for years, so I actually have great questions to ask.

教授问学生是不是在准备采访问题上遇到了麻烦，但学生回答说她有过这方面的经验，有很好的问题可以问。说明教授并没有理解该学生来找他的真正目的是什么。故本题答案为选项(B)。

Lecture 1(Q6–Q11)

讲座 || 人类学 • 世界上不同种类的历法

题目解析

6

What does the professor mainly discuss?

(A) ~~Various errors~~ in early calendars

(B) Why people came to believe that Earth moves around the Sun

(C) Examples of various types of calendars used in different cultures

(D) The belief that the position of planets and stars can predict future events

Professor

OK, I, **I want to begin today by talking about calendars.** I know, some of you are thinking it's not all that fascinating, right? But listen, the next time you look at a calendar, I want you to keep something in mind. There are at least three natural ways of measuring the...the passage of time—by day, by month, and by year.

7

The professor discusses various theories on how Stonehenge was used.

What can be inferred about the professor's opinion?

Not that different cultures haven't tried. Have any of you ever been to Stonehenge? No...you know, that amazing circle of giant stones in England? Well, if you ever go, and find yourself wondering why this culture way back in prehistoric England would go to so much work to construct

(A) She is sure Stonehenge was used as a calendar.

(B) She believes the main use for Stonehenge was probably as a temple or a tomb.

(C) She thinks that the stones were mainly used as a record of historical events.

(D) She admits that the purpose for which Stonehenge was constructed may never be known.

this monumental ring of enormous stones, ...well, **keep in mind that** a lot of us **think it was designed, at least partially, as a calendar**—to mark when the seasons of the year begin, according to the exact day when the Sun comes up from a particular direction. I have colleagues who insist it's a temple, maybe, or a tomb...**but they can't deny that it was also used as a calendar...probably to help figure out, for example, when farmers should begin their planting each year**.

8

According to the professor, how was the Mayan calendar mainly used?

(A) To keep track of long historical cycles

(B) To keep track of the lunar months

(C) To predict the outcome of royal decisions

(D) To allow priests to compare the orbits of Earth and Venus

The Mayans, in Central America, also invented a calendar, but for a different purpose. **The Mayans, especially the royalty and priests, wanted to look at long cycles of history**—so the calendar they used had to be able to count far into the future as well as far into the past. And not only were the Mayans keeping track of the natural timekeepers we mentioned before—Earth, the Moon, and the Sun—but another natural timekeeper: the planet Venus.

9

According to the professor, what was the basis of the ancient Chinese astrological cycle?

(A) The cycle of night and day

(B) The orbit of the Moon

(C) The cycle of the seasons

(D) The orbit of the planet Jupiter

Now, the ancient Chinese believed very strongly in astrology—the idea that you can predict future events based on the positions of the stars and planets like, say, Jupiter. Incidentally, **the whole Chinese system of astrology was based on the fact that the planet Jupiter goes around the Sun once every 12 years, so one orbit of Jupiter lasts 12 of our Earth years.** Apparently, that's why the Chinese calendar has a cycle of 12 years. You know, like, "The Year of the Dragon," "The Year of the Tiger," and so on...all parts of a 12-year astrological cycle, that we get from the orbit of Jupiter.

10

How did the Romans succeed in making their calendar more precise?

(A) By changing the number of weeks in a year

(B) By adding an extra day every four years

(C) By carefully observing the motion of the planet Jupiter

(D) By adopting elements of the Chinese calendar

So let's go right to the calendar that's now used throughout most of the world—a solar calendar—based on the number of days in a year. This calendar's mainly derived from the one the ancient Romans devised a couple thousand years ago. I mean, the Romans—with more than a little help from the Greeks—realized that a year actually lasts about 365 and one-quarter days. **And so they decided to round off most years to 365 days but make every fourth year into a leap year.** I mean, ...

11

How does the professor organize the lecture?

(A) By mentioning the problem of creating a calendar, then describing various attempts to deal with it

(B) By speaking of the modern calendar first, then comparing it with earlier ones

(C) By discussing how a prehistoric calendar was adapted by several different cultures

(D) By emphasizing the advantages and disadvantages of using various time cycles

本题相对比较特殊，考查全文结构。这种题型在真正的托福考试题中并不常见。在这个讲座中，教授先提到设计出一种精确的日历会遇到一系列的问题，接着又讲世界各种文化是如何克服这些问题的。故本题正确答案为选项(A)。

Lecture 2(Q12–Q16)

讲座 || 生物·海豚群体之间的交流方式

题目解析

12

What is the lecture mainly about?

(A) How dolphins produce the sounds they make

(B) How dolphins teach their young to identify signature whistles

(C) The professor's experience with dolphins on a research boat

(D) Various ways dolphins communicate with one another

Professor

We've been discussing animal communication. Um, today we're going to talk about dolphins. Now, dolphins make a wide range of communicative sounds and also display something called vocal learning, which is the ability of an animal to modify its vocalizations based on its experience with other animals.

13

According to a theory the professor mentions, why do dolphins travel side by side?

(A) To view each other's bubble streams

(B) To hear each other's signature whistles

In addition to whistles, dolphins produce clicks, which are actually sonar or sound waves. They use the clicks to communicate, but, more importantly, to navigate and hunt. How? Well, the sonar clicks bounce off objects, and then the dolphins convert the incoming signals into a three-dimensional picture...a, a mental

(C) To avoid interfering with other dolphins' sonar clicks

(D) To keep mothers close to their young

map…of what's around them. The clicks are extremely sensitive and accurate. The sonar clicks are also very strong. And there's this theory that, **one reason dolphins swim side by side is to avoid interference from each others' sonar clicks**. Interference would be confusing…it would prevent them from getting an accurate picture of their surroundings. Ah, and what's interesting is, dolphins will turn off their sonar when another dolphin passes in front.

14

What does the professor imply about bubble streams?

(A) They help protect dolphins from predators.

(B) Their function is similar to that of signature whistles.

(C) They do not appear to serve a communicative function.

(D) Dolphins use them to sense the movement of the water.

Male Student

In the book, it said that they also slap their tails against the water. Oh, and…the air that comes out when they breathe or whistle…the…ah…the bubble streams? They can control how the air bubbles come out. I thought that was really interesting.

Professor

Yes…the bubble streams are very interesting. **Dolphins can identify and locate each other by their bubble streams, and they can imitate the bubble stream patterns of other dolphins…sort of like saying hello. So as you can see, dolphins use many different sounds and behaviors to convey messages to each other.**

15

Why does the professor mention the time she spent on a boat doing research?

(A) To encourage students to do field-work

(B) To inform students about a paper she wrote

(C) To show how scientists collect data on marine life

(D) To illustrate that dolphins are difficult to locate

I'd like to tell you about when I was a graduate student...and...I spent one summer on a boat in the Atlantic Ocean studying marine life. One morning there were about 25 dolphins swimming with the boat. We could hear their clicks and whistles as they called to each other. Now, we were there as impartial scientists, to do research, but...how could we not notice the beauty as the bubble streams made patterns in the water and the dolphins appeared to dance and play? **It's wonderful when you do fieldwork and actually experience something you've been studying in a classroom. So if you ever have the opportunity...go for it.**

16

Listen again to part of the lecture.
Then answer the question.

What does this example illustrate?

(A) The differences between land and marine mammals

(B) The importance of burst pulses as a way dolphins communicate

Professor

And, members of the same family, their signature whistles have similar elements. **Dolphins use them as contact calls**—ah, they they call to each other while traveling and foraging. It helps keep the group together, and helps mothers and children find each other.

(C) One reason dolphins travel in large groups

(D) One way dolphins use signature whistles

Think of it like . . . ah, if you were traveling in the forest with one other person who was just out of sight, you'd call out, "Are you there?" and the other person would respond. But if there were several people in the forest, you would have to call that person's name to call to them.

Conversation 2(Q17–Q21)

对话 || 关于报名选修生物课

题目解析

17

Why does the student go to Professor Kirk's office?

(A) To find out if he needs to take a certain class to graduate

(B) To respond to Professor Kirk's invitation

(C) To ask Professor Kirk to be his advisor

(D) To ask Professor Kirk to sign a form

Student

Oh, unfortunately no. I have class this afternoon. And I was really hoping to talk to her today. **Hey, um, do you know if... she's accepting any more students into her introduction to Biology class?**

Employee

You want to know if you can take the class?

Student

Yes, if she's letting any more students sign up, I'd like, I'd like to join the class.

18

Why is the woman surprised at the man's request?

(A) He has not tried to sign up for Introduction to Biology at the registrar's office.

(B) He has waited until his senior year to take Introduction to Biology.

(C) A journalism student should not need a biology class.

(D) Professor Kirk no longer teaches Introduction to Biology.

Student

Yeah, that's why the registrar said it was full. I've got the form the registrar gave me, um, to get her permission to take the class. It's all filled out except for her signature. I'm hoping she'll let me in even though the class is full. **You see, I'm a senior this year, and, uh, ...this'll be my last semester, so it's my last chance...**

Employee

Oh, wow, really. <u>I mean</u> most students fulfill their science requirement the first year.

19

What does the man say about his advisor?

(A) She encouraged the man to take a science class.

(B) She encouraged the man to major in journalism.

(C) She is not aware of the man's problem.

(D) She thinks very highly of Professor Kirk.

Employee

Your advisor didn't say anything?

Student

Well, <u>to tell you the truth</u>, she's been after me to take a class like this for a while, but I'm double-majoring in art and journalism and so my schedule's been really tight with all the classes I gotta take, so somehow I never...

20

How will the man probably try to communicate his problem to Professor Kirk?

(A) By calling her

(B) By sending an email to her

(C) By leaving her a note

(D) By visiting her during office hours

Employee

Hmm. You know, not all professors check their emails regularly—I... I'm not sure if Professor Kirk does it or not. Here's an idea ...**<u>why don't you</u> stick a note explaining your situation under her door and ask her to call you if she needs more information?**

Student

Hey, that's a good idea, and then I can leave the form with you—if you still don't mind.

21

Listen again to part of the conversation.

Then answer the question.

Why does the man say this to the woman?

(A) To thank the woman for solving his problem

(B) To politely refuse the woman's suggestion

(C) To explain why he needs the woman's help

(D) To show that he understands that the woman is busy

Employee

Well, perhaps you could leave the form with me and I'll see if she'll sign it for you.

Student

You know, I appreciate that, but maybe I should explain the problem to her in person...

题目解析

22

What is the lecture mainly about?

(A) Various theories explaining why Mars cannot sustain life

(B) Various causes of geological changes on Mars

(C) The development of views about the nature of Mars

(D) Why it has been difficult to obtain information about Mars

教授讲了人类在不同时期探索火星所得到的数据，这表明人类对火星的认识是一直在变化的，故本题的正确答案为选项(C)。虽然从题型上来判断本题是主旨题，但其考查的实质内容是全文的逻辑结构。

23

According to the professor, what was concluded about Mars after the first spacecraft flew by it in 1965?

Professor

Well, it seems silly to us now, but those ideas were quite imaginative and, occasionally, scary in their time. Anyway, we began to rethink our image of Mars when the first spacecraft flew by the planet in 1965 and sent pictures back to Earth.

(A) It had few geological features of interest.

(B) It was similar to Earth but colder.

(C) It had at one time supported life.

(D) It had water under its surface.

Those pictures showed a planet that looked a lot more like our moon than Earth—lots of craters and not much else. It was bitterly cold, it had a very thin atmosphere, and that atmosphere was mostly carbon dioxide. So, the view of Mars after this first flyby mission was that dry, dead planet that Lisa mentioned.

24

What does the professor imply about conditions on Mars billions of years ago?

Choose 2 answers.

(A) Mars was probably even drier than it is today.

(B) The atmospheric pressure and the temperature may have been higher than they are today.

(C) Mars was inhabited by organisms that have since become fossilized.

(D) Large floods were shaping the planet's surface.

Mars had...has a lot more than craters—it has giant volcanoes and deep canyons. It also showed signs of dried-up riverbeds and plains that had been formed by massive floods. So we concluded that there must have been water on the planet at one time—billions of years ago. Now, what does it take for water to exist?

Male Student

You need to have a warm-enough temperature so that it doesn't freeze.

Professor

That's one thing—and the other is that you need enough atmospheric pressure, thick-enough air so that the water doesn't instantly vaporize. The Mars we see today doesn't have either of those conditions—it is too cold and the air is too thin—but **a long time ago, there may have been a thicker atmosphere that created a greenhouse effect that raised temperatures—and maybe that combination produced water on the surface of the planet.**

25

What is the possible significance of the gullies found on Mars in recent years?

(A) They may indicate current volcanic activity on Mars.

(B) They may indicate that the surface of Mars is becoming increasingly drier.

(C) They may indicate the current existence of water on Mars.

(D) They may hold fossils of organisms that once existed on Mars.

Professor

I'm not surprised. There're a lot of theories...a lot of speculation...and some argue the formations aren't caused by water at all. **But there're some ingenious theories that assume that there's a lot of water right under the planet's surface that somehow is causing the gullies to form.**

26

Listen again to part of the lecture. Then answer the question.

Why does the professor say this?

(A) To stress that Mars is ~~no longer interesting to explore~~

(B) To ~~describe items~~ that the spacecraft brought back from Mars

(C) To share ~~his interest in the study of fossils~~

(D) To show how much the view of Mars changed based on new evidence

Professor

So, maybe Mars wasn't just a dead, boring rock; maybe, it was, uh, a fascinating fossil that was once alive and dynamic—worthy of exploration.

27

Listen again to part of the lecture.

Then answer the question.

Why does the student say this?

(A) To ~~ask for clarification~~ of a previous statement

(B) To convey his opinion

(C) To rephrase ~~an earlier question~~

(D) To express ~~his approval~~

Male Student

I know; the planet was red and, uh, the people were green. I've seen some of those old movies. **What were they thinking?** I mean, really…they…

讲座 ‖ 历史·巨型雕塑的建筑意义

题目解析

28

What does the professor mainly discuss?

(A) The design and creation of the Statue of Liberty

(B) The creators of two colossal statues in the United States

(C) The purpose and symbolism of colossal statues

(D) The cost of colossal statues in ancient versus modern times

Now, it was one thing to build such statues, at an equally colossal cost, when the funds were being allocated by ancient kings and pharaohs. But if we're going to think about modern-day colossal statues, **we need to reexamine more closely their role as social and political symbols**, in order to understand why a society today—a society of free, taxpaying citizens—would agree to allocate so much of its resources to erecting them. A good example to start out with would be Mount Rushmore.

29

What evidence does the professor give that supports the idea that modern-day colossal statues are valued social and political symbols?

(A) They are very costly to build.

(B) They are studied in classrooms around the world.

(C) They are designed to last for thousands of years.

(D) They are inspired by great poetry.

Now, **it was one thing to build such statues, at an equally colossal cost,** when the funds were being allocated by ancient kings and pharaohs. **But if we're going to think about modern-day colossal statues, we need to reexamine more closely their role as social and political symbols, in order to understand why a society today—a society of free, tax-paying citizens—would agree to allocate so much of its resources to erecting them.** A good example to start out with would be Mount Rushmore.

30

According to the professor, what was one result of the Great Depression of the 1930s?

(A) International alliances eroded.

(B) Immigration to the United States increased.

(C) The public experienced a loss of confidence.

(D) The government could no longer provide funds for the arts.

Well, I personally think that the Great Depression of the 1930s actually makes this more understandable, not less so. Often it's the case that, precisely at times of hardship—when the very fabric of society seems to be unraveling and confidence is eroding—uh, **that people clamor for some public expression of strength and optimism, perhaps as a way of symbolizing its endurance in the face of difficulty.**

31

According to the professor, why did the state of South Dakota originally want to create a colossal monument?

(A) To generate income from tourism

(B) To symbolize the unity of society

(C) To commemorate the Great Depression

(D) To honor United States Presidents

So with that in mind, let's go back to Mount Rushmore. **__Actually__, the original motivation for a colossal monument in South Dakota had very little to do with all this symbolism...and everything to do with money:** you see, it was first conceived of basically as a tourist attraction, and it was supposed to feature the images of legendary figures of the American West, like the explorers Lewis and Clark. The government of South Dakota thought it would bring lots of money into the state.

32

Why does the professor discuss the poem by Emma Lazarus?

(A) To emphasize the close relationship between literature and sculpture

(B) To illustrate how the meaning associated with a monument can change

(C) To stress the importance of the friendship between France and the United States

(D) To point out a difference between Mount Rushmore and the Statue of Liberty

But the shift in the statue's meaning started soon after it was built. Back in 1883, Emma Lazarus wrote that famous poem—you know, the one that goes: "Give me your tired, your poor..." and so on and so forth. That poem describes the Statue of Liberty as a beacon of welcome for the entire world. Well, in the early 1900s, it was put on a plaque on the pedestal that the Statue of Liberty stands on.

33

Listen again to part of the lecture.

Then answer the question.

What does the professor imply about the poem by Emma Lazarus?

(A) It is one of his favorite poems.

(B) Few people have read the entire poem.

(C) He does not need to recite the full text of the poem.

(D) Lazarus was not able to complete the poem.

But the shift in the statue's meaning started soon after it was built. **Back in 1883, Emma Lazarus wrote that famous poem—you know, the one that goes: "Give me your tired, your poor..." and so on and so forth.** That poem describes the Statue of Liberty as a beacon of welcome for the entire world. Well, in the early 1900s, it was put on a plaque on the pedestal that the Statue of Liberty stands on.

Authentic TOEFL Practice Test 3

Conversation 1(Q1–Q5)

对话 ‖ 关于一堂物理课被取消

题目解析

1

Why does the woman come to the office?

(A) To notify the university of her change of address

(B) To find out where her physics class is being held

(C) To get directions to the science building

(D) To complain about her physics class's being canceled

Female student

Excuse me, uh, I'm supposed to be having my physics class in the science building, but no one's in the classroom...**Could you tell me where the class is?** Physics 403? Has it been moved?

Receptionist

Well, there's a room assignment sheet on the bulletin board outside this office...

2

What happened to the letter the university sent to the woman?

(A) She threw it away by mistake

(B) Her roommate forgot to give it to her

(C) It was sent to her old mailing address

(D) It was sent to another student by mistake

Female student

Woodhouse. Laura Woodhouse.

Receptionist

OK, ummm, Woodhouse...let me see...ah, it says here we sent it to your apartment on...uh...Center Street.

Student

Oh, that's my old apartment...I moved out of there a little while ago...

Receptionist

Well...and **I suppose you haven't changed your mailing address at the administration office.** Well, that would explain it.

3

Why was the woman's physics class canceled?

(A) Not enough students signed up to take the class.

(B) No professors were available to teach the class.

(C) The university changed its requirements for physics students.

(D) There were no classrooms available in the science building at that hour.

Female student

Yeah, I guess that's it. But, how can they cancel a class after offering it? If I'd known this was gonna happen, I would have taken it last semester.

Receptionist

I know, it's really inconvenient for you; I understand that, but, um…**if we don't have enough students signed up for the course, the college can't offer it.** You know, it's, um, a practical issue, like, we can't have an instructor when there're only a few students in the class. You see what I mean?

4

What does the man suggest the woman do before the beginning of next semester?

(A) Consult with her advisor about her class schedule

(B) Check with the registrar's office about the location of the class

(C) Register for her classes early

(D) Call the physics department

Receptionist

Well, it depends on the class, but for that class, you have to have…um…let's see… usually it'd be at least ten people, but since it was canceled this semester, they might even do it with less. But you know what you should do? **Give the physics department a call a couple of weeks before the semester starts.** They'll be able to tell you if they're planning to go through with it… It's their decision, actually.

5

Listen again to part of the conversation.
Then answer the question.

What does the man imply when he says this?

(A) He knows the physics class has been canceled.

(B) He is not sure where the science building is.

(C) Many of the room assignments have been changed.

(D) **The women can check for herself where her class is.**

Female student

Excuse me, uh, I'm supposed to be having my physics class in the science building, but no one's in the classroom...Could you tell me where the class is? Physics 403? Has it been moved?

Receptionist

Well, there's a room assignment sheet on the bulletin board outside this office...

学生向工作人员询问物理课上课的地点在哪里，工作人员直接回答："公告栏里有教室分配表……"。这表明，工作人员认为学生可以自己去解决这个问题，他没必要对这个问题给予明确的回答。故选项(D)为正确答案。

Lecture 1(Q6–Q11)

讲座 || 环境科学 · 人类活动对蜂鸟栖息地的破坏

题目解析

6

What does the professor mainly discuss?

(A) Major changes in the migratory patterns of hummingbirds

(B) The adaptation of hummingbirds to urban environments

(C) Concern about the reduction of hummingbird habitat

(D) The impact of ecotourism on hummingbird populations

Professor

Now, we've been talking about the loss of animal habitat from housing developments, uh, growing cities...small habitat losses. **But today I want to begin talking about what happens when habitat is reduced across a large area.** There are, of course, animal species that require large areas of habitat...and, um, some migrate over very long distances. **So what's the impact of habitat loss on those animals? Animals that need large areas of habitat?**

Well, I'll use the hummingbirds as an example. Now, you know a hummingbird is amazingly small...

"We've been talking about..."这句话说明教授之前所讲的内容，听到这种句式时，考生不用进行记录，因为托福考试中一般只会问这次课的主要内容是什么。应该注意听教授下面所说的话"But today I want to begin talking about..."，这才是这节课的主要内容，也是这道题的答案所在。

7

What does the professor imply might cause a decrease in the hummingbird population?

(A) An increase in the ecotourism industry

(B) An increase in the use of land to raise crops and cattle

(C) A decrease in banding studies

(D) A decrease in the distance traveled during migration

But the problem, well…**as natural habitat along these migration routes is developed by humans for housing or agriculture, or, um, cleared for raising cattle, for instance…there's less food available for migrating hummingbirds.** Their nesting sites are affected, too…the same…by the same sorts of human activities. **And all of these activities pose a real threat to the hummingbird population.**

8

What does the professor say people have done to help hummingbirds survive?

(A) They have built a series of hummingbird feeding stations.

(B) They have supported new laws that punish polluters of wildlife habitats.

(C) They have replanted native flowers in once polluted areas.

(D) They have learned to identify various hummingbird species.

So, to help them survive, we need to preserve their habitats…And one of the concrete ways people have been doing this is by cleaning up polluted habitat areas…and then **replanting flowers, uh, replanting native flowers that hummingbirds feed on.** Promoting ecological tourism is another way to help save their habitat. As the number of visitors—ecotourists who come to hummingbird habitats to watch the birds—the more the number of visitors grows, the more local businesses profit. So ecological tourism can bring financial rewards. All the more reason to value these beautiful little creatures and their habitat, right?

教授先说了replanting flowers，紧接着又重说了一遍replanting native flowers，很明显这是在强调native的重要性。听力中遇到这种强调性内容时要多加注意，经常会成为考点。

9

What way of collecting information about migrating hummingbirds does the professor mention?

(A) Receiving radio signals from electronic tracking devices

(B) Being contacted by people who recapture banded birds

(C) Counting the birds that return to the same region every year

(D) Comparing old and young birds' migration routes

And, then we place an extremely lightweight band around one of its legs...well, what looks like a leg—although, technically it's considered part of the bird's foot. Anyway, these bands are perfectly safe. And some hummingbirds have worn them for years with no evidence of any problems. The band is labeled with a tracking number... oh, and **there is a phone number on the band for people to call, for free, to report a banded bird to be found or recaptured. So when a banded bird is recaptured and reported,** we learn about its migration route, its growth...and how long it has been alive...its lifespan. One recaptured bird had been banded almost 12 years earlier! she was one of the oldest humming birds on record.

Another interesting thing we've learned is...that some hummingbirds, uh, they no longer use a certain route; they travel by a different route to reach their destination.

10

What does the professor imply researchers have learned while studying hummingbird migration?

So when a banded bird is recaptured and reported, we learn about its migration route, its growth...and how long it has been alive...its lifespan. One recaptured bird had

(A) Hummingbirds have totally disappeared from some countries due to recent habitat destruction.

(B) Programs to replant flowers native to hummingbird habitats are not succeeding.

(C) Some groups of hummingbirds have changed their migration patterns.

(D) Some plant species pollinated by hummingbirds have become extinct.

been banded almost 12 years earlier! She was one of the oldest hummingbirds on record.

Another interesting thing we've learned is…that some hummingbirds, uh, they no longer use a certain route. They travel by a different route to reach their destination.

"Another interesting thing..." 听到这样的表达时，要注意其后面的内容，这些内容经常成为考点。

11

Listen again to part of the lecture.

Then answer the question.

What does the professor imply when she says this?

(A) There is disagreement about the idea she has presented.

(B) She does not plan to discuss all the details.

(C) Her next point may seem to contradict what she has just said.

(D) The point she will make next should be obvious to the student.

So hummingbirds have to rely on plants in their natural habitat. **And it goes without saying,** but…well, the opposite is true as well. Plants depend on hummingbirds too.

"it goes without saying..." 是"不言自明"的意思。故选项(D)为正确答案。

Lecture 2(Q12–Q17)

讲座 || 电影史・一位早期电影制作人的电影风格

题目解析

12

What is the main purpose of the lecture?

(A) To discuss the style of an early film-maker

(B) To describe different types of filmmaking in the 1930s

(C) To discuss the emergence of the documentary film

(D) To describe Painlevé's influence on today's science-fiction films

Professor

Okay, we've been discussing films in the 1920s and '30s, and, ah, how back then, film categories as we know them today had not yet been established. We, ah, said that, by today's standards, many of the films of the '20s and '30s would be considered "hybrids"; that is, a mixture of styles that wouldn't exactly fit into any of today's categories. And in that context, **today we are going to talk about a, a film-maker who began making very unique films in the late 1920s.** He was French, and his name was Jean Painlevé.

Jean Painlevé was born in 1902. He made his first film in 1928. Now, in a way, Painlevé's films conform to norms of the '20s and '30s; that is, they don't fit very neatly into the categories we use to classify films today. That said, even by the standards of the '20s and '30s, Painlevé's films were a unique hybrid of styles. He had a special way of fusing—or, or some people might say confusing—science and fiction.

同之前所讲，“We've been discussing...”介绍的是上节课的内容，了解即可。“today we are going to talk about...”才是本节课的主要内容，必须认真听，这通常是主旨题的出处。

13

Why are Painlevé's films typical of the films of the 1920s and 1930s?

(A) They do not have sound.

(B) They are filmed underwater.

(C) They are easy to understand.

(D) They are difficult to categorize.

Today we are going to talk about a, a filmmaker who began making very unique films in the late 1920s. He was French, and his name was Jean Painlevé.

Jean Painlevé was born in 1902. He made his first film in 1928. **Now, in a way, Painlevé's films conform to norms of the '20s and '30s; that is, they don't fit very neatly into the categories we use to classify films today.** That said, even by the standards of the '20s and '30s, Painlevé's films were a unique hybrid of styles. He had a special way of fusing—or, or some people might say confusing—science and fiction...

14

According to the professor, how did Painlevé's film confuse the audience?

(A) They show animals out of their natural habitat .

But then he'd suddenly change the image or narration to remind us how different the animals are, how unlike humans. **He**

(B) They depict animals as having both human and animal characteristics.

(C) The narration is scientific and difficult to understand.

(D) The audiences of the 1920s and 1930s were not used to films shot underwater.

confused his audience in the way he portrayed the animals he filmed, mixing up our notions of the categories "humans" and "animals." The films make us a little uncomfortable at times because we are uncertain about what we are seeing. It gives him films an uncanny feature…the familiar made unfamiliar, the normal made suspicious. He liked twists; he liked the unusual. In fact, one of his favorite sea animals was the sea horse because with sea horses, it's the male that gets pregnant, it's the male that carries the babies. And he thought that was great. His first and most celebrated underwater film is about the sea horse.

15

Why does the professor mention sea horses?

(A) To explain that they were difficult to film in the 1930s

(B) To point out that Cousteau made documentaries about them

(C) To illustrate Painlevé's fascination with unusual animals

(D) To explain why Painlevé's underwater films were not successful

But then he'd suddenly change the image or narration to remind us how different the animals are, how unlike humans. He confused his audience in the way he portrayed the animals he filmed, mixing up our notions of the categories **"humans" and "animals."** The films make us a little uncomfortable at times because we are uncertain about what we are seeing. **It gives him films an uncanny feature…the familiar made unfamiliar, the normal made suspicious. He liked twists; he liked the unusual.** In fact, one of his favorite sea animals was the seahorse because with sea horses, it's the male that gets pregnant, it's the male that carries the babies. And he thought that was great. His first and most celebrated underwater film is about the sea horse.

16

Why does the professor compare the film style of Jacques Cousteau and Jean Painlevé?

(A) To explain how Painlevé influenced Cousteau

(B) To emphasize the uniqueness of Painlevé's filming style

(C) To emphasize the artistic value of Cousteau's documentary films

(D) To demonstrate the superiority of Painleve's filmmaking equipment

Professor

Ah, Jacques Cousteau. Well, Painlevé and Cousteau did both film underwater, and they were both innovators, so you are right in that sense, **but that's pretty much where the similarities end.** First of all, Painlevé was about 20 years ahead of Cousteau...Um, and Cousteau's adventures were high-tech, with lots of fancy equipment, **whereas** Painlevé kind of patched the equipment together as he needed it...Uh, Cousteau usually filmed large animals, usually in the open sea, **whereas** Painlevé generally filmed smaller animals, and he liked to film in shallow water...Uh, what else? Well, **the main difference** was that Cousteau simply investigated and presented the facts; he, he didn't mix in fiction. He was a strict documentarist; he set the standard, really, for the nature documentary. Painlevé, **on the other hand**, as we said before, mixed in elements of fiction, and his films are much more artistic, incorporating music as an important element.

17

Listen again to part of the lecture.

Then answer the question.

What does the student imply when he says this?

(A) He does not like Jean Painleve's films.

(B) He thinks that the professor should spend more time discussing Jacques Cousteau's film.

(C) He believes that high-quality film-makers are usually well known.

(D) He believes that Jean Painleve's films have been unfairly overlooked.

Student 2

Well, maybe I shouldn't be asking this... Uh, but if Painlevé's films are so special, so good, why haven't we ever heard of them? I mean, everyone's heard of Jacques Cousteau...

Conversation 2(Q18–Q22)

对话 ‖ 关于校园考古志愿者的招聘

题目解析

18

Why does the student go to see the professor?

(A) To ask about a class assignment

(B) To find out about a mid-semester project

(C) To get information about summer jobs

(D) To discuss ways to improve his grade

Male Student

Hi, Professor Archer. **You know how in class last week you said that you were looking for students who were interested in volunteering for your archaeology project?**

Professor

Of course. Are you volunteering?

Male Student

Yes, I am. It sounds really interesting. But, ummm, do I need to have any experience with these kinds of projects?

Professor

No, not really. I assume that most students taking the introductory-level class will have little or no experience with archaeological research, but that's OK.

Male Student

Oh, good—that's a relief. Actually, that's why I'm volunteering for the project—to get experience. What kind of work is it?

19

What was originally located on the site of the lecture hall?

(A) A farmhouse

(B) A pottery factory

(C) A clothing store

(D) A bottle-manufacturing plant

Professor

Well, as you know, we're studying the history of the campus this semester. This used to be an agricultural area and **we already know that where the main lecture hall now stands there once were a farmhouse and barn that were erected in the late 1700s.** We are excavating near the lecture hall to see what types of artifacts we find—you know, things people used in the past that got buried when the campus was constructed. We've already begun to find some very interesting items like, um, old bottles, buttons, pieces of clay pottery…

20

What is mentioned as an advantage of working on this project?

(A) Off-campus travel is paid off.

(B) Students can leave class early.

(C) The location is convenient.

(D) It fulfills a graduation requirement.

Professor

That's just one of the questions we hope to answer with this project.

Male Student

Wow—and it's all right here on campus...

Professor

That's right, no traveling involved. I wouldn't expect volunteers to travel to a site, especially in the middle of the semester. We expect to find many more things, but we do need more people to help.

21

What is the professor considering doing to get move volunteers?

(A) Offering extra class credit

(B) Paying the students for their time

(C) Asking for student volunteers from outside her class

(D) Providing flexible work schedules

Male Student

Sounds like it could be a lot of work. Is there...umm...is there any way I can use the experience to get some extra credit in class? I mean can I write a paper about it?

Professor

I think it'll depend on what type of work you do in the excavation, but I imagine we can arrange something. Well, actually, **I've been considering offering extra credit for class** because I've been having a tough time getting volunteers...Extra credit is always a good incentive for students.

22

What information does the student still need to get from the professor?

(A) The name of the senior researcher

(B) What book he needs to read before the next lecture

(C) When the train session will be scheduled

(D) Where the project is located

Male Student

Sure, I know John. By the way, **will there be some sort of training?**

Professor

Yes, uh, **I wanna wait till Friday to see how many students volunteer. And then I'll schedule a training class next week at a time that's convenient for everyone.**

Student

Ok, I'll wait to hear from you. Thanks a lot for accepting me!

Lecture 3(Q23–Q28)

讲座 ‖ 美术史 · 最古老的洞穴壁画

题目解析

23

What does the professor mainly discuss?

(A) The oldest known cave art

(B) How ancient cave art is dated

(C) The homes of Paleolithic humans

(D) How Paleolithic humans thought about animals

Professor

Some of the world's oldest preserved art is the cave art of Europe, most of it in Spain and France. And, uh, the earliest cave paintings found to date are those of the Chauvet Cave in France, discovered in 1994.

24

Why does the professor mention his daughter?

(A) To describe her reaction to seeing the paintings

(B) To explain the universal appeal of the Chauvet paintings

(C) To demonstrate the size of most Paleolithic cave art

(D) To emphasize his point about the age of the Chauvet paintings

And, you know, I remember when I heard about the results of the dating of the Chauvet paintings. I said to my wife, "Can you believe these paintings are over 30,000 years old?" and my three-year-old daughter piped up and said, "Is that older than my great-grandmother?" **That was the oldest age she knew. And, you know, come to think of it. It's pretty hard for me to really understand how long 30,000 years is too.** I mean, we tend to think the people who lived at that time must have been pretty primitive…but I'm gonna show you some slides in a few minutes, and I think you'll agree with me that this art is anything but primitive—they're are masterpieces. And they look so real, so alive, that it's very hard to imagine that they are so very old.

25

What is the professor's opinion about the art at the Chauvet cave?

(A) It is extremely well done.

(B) It probably reflected artists' religious beliefs.

(C) It is less sophisticated than the art at Lascaux and Altamira.

(D) It is probably not much older than the art at Lascaux and Altamira.

And, you know, I remember when I heard about the results of the dating of the Chauvet paintings. I said to my wife, "Can you believe these paintings are over 30,000 years old?" and my three-year-old daughter piped up and said, "Is that older than my great-grandmother?" That was the oldest age she knew. And, you know, come to think of it. It's pretty hard for me to really understand how long 30,000 years is too. I mean, we tend to think that people who lived at that time must have been pretty primitive…**but I'm gonna show you some slides in a few minutes, and I think you'll agree with me that this art is anything but primitive—they are masterpieces.** And they look so real, so alive, that it's very hard to imagine that they're so very old.

注意：anything but... = not...at all

26

According to the professor, what is the significance of charcoal marks on the walls of the Chauvet cave?

(A) They suggest that Paleolithic people cooked their food in the cave.

(B) They prove that people came to the cave long after the paintings were made.

(C) They show how much light the Paleolithic artists needed for their work.

(D) They were used in recent times to date the paintings.

And people did go see the art—there are charcoal marks from their torches on the cave walls, clearly dating from thousands of years after the paintings were made—so we can tell people went there. They came, but they didn't stay. Deep inside a cave like that is not really a place you'd want to stay, so, uh, why? What inspired the Paleolithic artists to make such beautiful art in such inaccessible places? We'll never really know, of course, though it's interesting to speculate.

27

Compared with other Paleolithic art, what is unusual about the animals painted at Chauvet?

(A) Most of them are horses.

(B) Many of them are dangerous.

(C) Many of them are shown alongside humans.

(D) All of them are species that are still found in France.

But, uh…getting to the paintings themselves. Virtually all Paleolithic cave art represents animals, and Chauvet is no exception. The artists were highly skilled at using—or even enhancing—the natural shape of the cave walls to give depth and perspectives to their drawings, the sense of motion and vitality in these animals—well, wait till I show you the slides. Anyway, most Paleolithic cave art depicts large herbivores. Horses are most common overall, with deer and bison pretty common too, probably animals they hunted. **But earlier at Chauvet, there is a significant interest in large, dangerous animals. Lots of rhinoceroses, lions, mammoths, bears…**

28

What are two questions about the Chauvet cave artists that the professor raises but cannot answer?

Choose 2 answers.

(A) How they lighted their work area

(B) How they obtained pigments for their paints

(C) Why they chose to paint certain animals and not others

(D) Why they placed their art in dark, uninhabited places

...They came, but they didn't stay. Deep inside a cave like that is not really a place you'd want to stay, so uh, **why? What inspired the Paleolithic artists to make such beautiful art in such inaccessible places?** We'll never know, of course, though it's interesting to speculate.

Remember that the ranges of many animal species were different back then, so all these animals actually lived in the region at that time—but, uh, the Chauvet artists didn't paint people. There is a half-man, half-bison creature, and there is outlines of human hands but no depiction of a full human.

So, why these precise animals? Why not birds...fish...snakes? Was it for their religion? magic? Or sheer beauty? We don't know. But whatever it was, it was worth it to them to spend hours deep inside a cave, with just a torch between them and utter darkness. So, on that note, let's dim the lights, so we can see these slides and actually look at the techniques they used.

Lecture 4(Q29–Q34)

讲座 || 天文学·如何识别星球上的化学成分

题目解析

29

What is the lecture mainly about?

(A) Different ways of magnifying the spectrum of a star

(B) How a chemical element was first discovered on the Sun

(C) How astronomers identify the chemical elements in a star

(D) Why the spectra of different stars are composed of different colors

Professor

Now, astronomy didn't really, uh, balloon into the science it is today until the development of spectroscopy. Spectroscopy is basically the study of spectra and spectral lines of light, and specifically for us, the light from stars. **It makes it possible to analyze the light emitted from stars. When you analyze this light, you can figure out their distance from the Earth, and identify what they are made of—determine their chemical composition.**

Before we get into that, though, it's probably a good thing to back up a bit. You all know how when you take a crystal prism and pass a beam of sunlight through it, you get a spectrum which looks like a continuous band of rainbow colors. The light that we see with our human eyes as a band of rainbow color falls in a range of what's called visible light. And visible light spectroscopy is probably the most important kind of spectroscopy.

Anyone wanna take a stab at the scientific term for visible light?...And I'm sure all of you know this because you all did the reading for today...

30

What does the professor explain to one of the students about the term "radiation"?

(A) It is defined incorrectly in the textbooks.

(B) It was first used in the nineteenth century.

(C) It is rarely used by astronomers.

(D) It does not refer only to harmful energy.

Female Student

Optical radiation. **But I thought being exposed to radiation is dangerous.**

Professor

Yes and no. If you are talking about radiation like in the element uranium, yeah, that's dangerous. But radiation as a general term actually refers to anything that spreads away from its source, so optical radiation is just visible light energy spreading out.

OK, so we've got a spectrum of a beam of sunlight and it looks like the colors bleed into each other; uh, there are no interruptions, just a band flowing from violet to green to yellow to...you get the idea.

31

What can be inferred about two stars if their spectra have similar spectral line patterns?

(A) The stars are approximately the same distance from the Earth.

Well, what happens if the sunlight spectrum is magnified? Maybe you all didn't do the reading. Well, here's what you'd see. I want you to notice that this spectrum is interrupted by dark lines, called spectral lines. If you really magnified the spectrum of the sunlight, you could identify more than 100,000 of them. They may look kind

(B) The stars probably have some chemical elements in common.

(C) The stars have nearly the same brightness.

(D) The stars are probably of the same size.

of randomly placed, but they actually form many distinct patterns. And if you were looking at the spectrum of some other star, the colors would be the same, **but the spectral lines would break it up at different places, making different patterns. Each pattern stands for a distinct chemical element, and so different sets or patterns of spectral lines mean that the star has a different chemical composition.**

32

According to the professor, what is the purpose of heating an element in a spectroscopic flame test?

(A) To cause an element to emit light

(B) To study an element in combination with other elements

(C) To remove impurities from the element

(D) To measure an element's resistance to heat

Professor

Well, a kind of spectroscopic library of elements was compiled using flame tests. A known element—uh, say a piece of iron, for example—is heated in a pure gas flame. The iron eventually heats to the point that it radiates light. This light is passed through a prism, which breaks it up into a spectrum, and a unique pattern, kind of like a chemical fingerprint, of spectral lines for that element appears. This process was repeated over and over again for many different elements. So we can figure out the chemical makeup of another star by comparing the spectral pattern it has to the pattern of the elements in the library.

33

Listen again to part of the lecture.

Then answer the question.

Why does the professor say this?

(A) He is about to provide some background information.

(B) He is about to repeat what he just said.

(C) He intends to focus on the history of astronomy.

(D) He intends to explain two different points of view.

Before we get into that, though, it's probably a good thing to back up a bit. You all know how when you take a crystal prism and pass a beam of sunlight through it, you get a spectrum which looks like a continuous band of rainbow colors. The light that we see with our human eyes as a band of rainbow color falls in a range of what's called visible light. And visible light spectroscopy is probably the most important kind of spectroscopy.

Anyone wanna to take a stab at the scientific term for visible light?...And I'm sure all of you know this because you all did the reading for today...

34

Listen again to part of the lecture.

Then answer the question.

Why does the professor ask this?

(A) To check the students' understanding of their reading assignment

Oh! An interesting story about how one of the elements was discovered through spectroscopy.There was a pretty extensive library of spectral line patterns of elements even by the 1860s. A British astronomer was analyzing a spectrograph of sunlight, and he noticed a particular pattern of spectral lines that didn't match anything in the library. So he put two

(B) To give the students a hint to the answer to his previous question

(C) To emphasize how important it is for astronomers to study Greek

(D) To remind the students about the historical background of astronomy

and two together, and decided there was an element in the Sun that hadn't been discovered here on the Earth yet. Any guesses about what that element is? It actually turned out to be pretty common, and I'm sure all of you know it. OK. Let's try something else. **Any of you happen to be familiar with the Greek word for Sun by chance?**

TOEFL iBT READING

托福考试官方指南解析

阅读部分

Reading Practice Sets

Practice Set 1

THE ORIGINS OF CETACEANS

文章结构

标 题	鲸的起源
第一段	鲸类动物是哺乳动物，最近发现了介于鲸类动物和陆地哺乳动物之间的中间或者过渡物种。
第二段	1979年，在巴基斯坦发现了迄今最古老的鲸类化石，命名为*Pakicetus*。
第三段	1979年出土化石的特征。
第四段	1989年，在埃及发现了另一种早期鲸类动物的化石*Basilosaurus*，比*Pakicetus*年代晚。
第五段	1994年，在巴基斯坦又发现了一种古鲸类，名为*Ambulocetus*，年代介于前两种之间。

题目解析

1

关键词：presence of a blowhole, cetaceans

定位句：Their streamlined bodies, the absence of hind legs, and the presence of a fluke and blowhole cannot disguise their affinities with land-dwelling mammals.

解题方法：直选法

(B) It cannot conceal the fact that cetaceans are mammals.

在这个选项中conceal = disguise，符合细节题正确选项的特征：正确答案为原文定位句的同义转述。

错误选项讲解：

(A) It ~~clearly~~ indicates that cetaceans are mammals.

此选项极容易被误选。它来自本段的第一句话，但该句话并不包含本题出题点中的另一个关键词presence of a blowhole，也就是说，它并不是presence of a blowhole所说明的问题。另外，这个选项中程度副词clearly用词错误，因为原文中并没有这样的程度副词出现。

> 程度副词的误用是许多错误选项共同的特征。

(C) It is the main difference between cetaceans and land-dwelling mammals.

注意原文和选项中意思的对应：原文讲的是cetaceans与land-dwelling mammals之间有affinities，这是两者之间的相似点similarities，并不是differences，所以此选项必错。

> 注意：对于该选项，判断思路非常重要。它要求考生在单词词义之间建立起对应关系。掌握这种思路有助于考生在考试中迅速找出正确选项或是排除错误选项，从而节省做题时间，并且提高正确率。

> 思路关联
>
> 选项(A)的错误思路也出现在本文第七题选项(C)，练习五第一题选项(A)中。
>
> 选项(C)的思路也可见于练习三第七题选项(A)和练习六第三题选项(D)。

2

关键词：early sea otters

定位句：However, **unlike** the cases of sea otters and pinnipeds(...), it is not easy to envision what the first whales looked like.

解题方法：直选法

(A) It is not difficult to imagine what they looked like.

此题采用一种“取非”的思路。这种思路简化为如下结构：

“取非”思路简化图

原文：Unlike a, b 有 c 的特征 → 答案：a 无 c 的特征。

原文说：“与sea otters and pinnipeds的情况不一样，想要知道早期whales的样子是一件很不容易的事情。答案(A) 采用“取非”思路可得出：“想要知道早期sea otters的样子是一件不难的事情。”

思路关联

练习三的第六题也采用了“取非”的思路解题。

3

PRECIOUS

If you say that something such as a resource is **precious**, you mean that it is valuable and should not be wasted or used badly.

同义词: valuable, costly, expensive, priceless

EXACT

Exact means correct in every detail. For example, an exact copy is the same in every detail as the thing it is copied from.

同义词: accurate, correct, precise, definite

SCARCE

If something is **scarce**, there is not enough of it.

同义词: rare, few, infrequent, insufficient, in short supply

VALUABLE

If you describe something or someone as **valuable**, you mean that they are very useful and helpful.

同义词: precious, costly, expensive, useful, helpful, beneficial

INITIAL

You use **initial** to describe something that happens at the beginning of a process.

同义词: first, beginning, incipient, primary, introductory

通过上面五个单词的意义对比，可以得出与precious意义最接近的是选项(C) valuable。

4

关键词：*Pakicetus*, cetaceans, similar

定位句：Although limited to a skull, the *Pakicetus* fossil provides precious details on the origins of cetaceans. The skull is cetacean-like but...

解题方法：直选法

(C) skull shapes

原文已经指明：skull是像cetacean的。

5

指代题：答案为选项(A) *Pakicetus*

定位句：It has been suggested that ***Pakicetus*** fed on fish in shallow water and was not yet adapted for life in the open ocean. **It** probably bred and gave birth on land.

译文：据推测，*Pakicetus*生活在浅水中，以鱼为主要食物，它们还没有完全适应广阔海域的水生环境。它们很有可能是在陆地上产仔的。

6

EXPOSE

To **expose** something that is usually hidden means to uncover it so that it can be seen.

同义词: uncover, display, exhibit, present, reveal, show, unveil

EXPLAIN

① If you **explain** something, you give details about it or describe it so that it can be understood.

② If you **explain** something that has happened, you give people reasons for it, especially in an attempt to justify it.

同义词: give a reason for, account for, justify, clarify, describe

VISIBLE

If something is **visible**, it can be seen.

同义词: observable, unconcealed, apparent, clear, evident

IDENTIFY

① If you **identify** something, you discover or notice its existence.

② If you can **identify** someone or something, you are able to recognize them or distinguish them from others.

③ If you **identify** someone or something, you name them or say who or what they are.

同义词: recognize, diagnose, name

LOCATE

① If you **locate** something or someone, you find out where they are.

② If you **locate** something in a particular place, you put it there or build it there.

同义词: find, detect, discover, put, settle

通过上面五个单词的意义对比，可以得出与exposed意义最接近的是选项(B) visible。

另外，大家还需要记住：

【考】expose to = subject to

【英】to cause (someone) to experience something or to be influenced or affected by something

【汉】*v.* 使处于…的影响之下

【预】make vulnerable, imperil, leave open

【例】The workers were **exposed** to dangerous chemicals.

注意：【考】列举了TOEFL真题中曾经出现过的考点。

【预】预测未来考点，即后面所列的词汇也可能成为考点，且与此题所考单词的意思一致。

7

关键词：the hind leg of *Basilosaurus*

定位句：..., a complete hind leg that features a foot with three tiny toes. Such legs would have been far too small to have supported the 50-foot-long *Basilosaurus* on land.

译文：……一条完整的后题，上面长有一只脚，脚上只有三个小小的脚趾头。这样的后腿太小了，它们没办法在陆地上支撑50英尺高的*Basilosaurus*。

解题方法：直选法

(D) could not have walked on land.

既然后腿没办法在陆地上支撑*Basilosaurus*，那*Basilosaurus*就自然无法在陆地上行走。故本题的正确答案为选项(D)。

错误选项讲解：

(A) lived later than ~~*Ambulocetus natans*~~

原文第五段的确指出*Ambulocetus* natans lived 9 million years before *Basilosaurus*，但第五段并不是本题的出题段落。本题的出题点是the hind leg of *Basilosaurus*说明了什么问题，所以只能从第四段关于the hind leg of *Basilosaurus* 的部分中寻找本题答案。

简捷思路：由于*Ambulocetus natans*并不是本题定位句所涉及的内容，因此不作为考虑对象，可直接忽略。

(B) lived at the same time as ~~*Pakicetus*~~

作者在本段中明确指出*Basilosaurus* lived around 40 million years ago, 12 million years after *Pakicetus*，而此选项却说*Basilosaurus*与*Pakicetus*生存在相同的时期，必然错误。

简捷思路：由于*Pakicetus*并不是本题定位句所涉及的内容，因此不作为考虑对象，可直接忽略。

(C) was able to swim ~~well~~

程度副词well修饰错误。从本段信息只能得出*Basilosaurus*生活在水里，并没有任何信息能够推断出*Basilosaurus*在水里游泳游得well。此选项的错误方式在本文第一题(A)选项的讲解中已经进行了详细的阐述。

选项陷阱

有些选项虽然在原文中出现了，但由于不是出题点所涉及的内容，所以仍然不能成为正确选项。这类选项是ETS在TOEFL阅读试题中经常设置的一种迷惑性选项。所以，在选项中若发现出题点并未涉及的内容，可直接跳过该选项，不予考虑。

思路关联

此题中迷惑选项(A)的思路与练习六第十题选项(D)类似。

8

关键词：*Basilosaurus* bred and gave birth

定位句：*Basilosaurus* was undoubtedly a <u>fully marine whale</u> with possibly nonfunctional, or vestigial, hind legs.

解题方法：直选法

(D) In a marine environment

此选项与原文中的fully marine whale相对应。

错误选项讲解：

原文只说*Basilosaurus*是海里的鲸鱼，并不能由此得出浅水（shallow water）里产仔（bred and gave birth）的结论，故选项(C)错误。其实这是将*Pakicetus*的信息混杂后错误地安在了Basilosaurus身上，文中第三段指出，*Pakicetus*在浅水中捕食鱼类，但是在陆地上产仔。

9

定位句：The fossil luckily includes a good portion of the hind legs.

解题方法：排除法

(A) Fossil legs of early whales ~~are a rare find~~.

(C) The discovery allowed scientists to ~~reconstruct a complete skeleton of the whale~~.

(D) Until that time, only the ~~front legs~~ of early whales had been discovered.

这三个选项加删除线的部分均不是原文所论述的内容，故均可排除。

(B) The legs provided important information about the evolution of cetaceans.

该选项与原文主旨内容evolution of cetaceans相关，所以在排除(A)(C)(D)三个选项后，可断定它为正确答案。

10

句子简化题

原文中的考点有明确的逻辑关系，因此可以按照以下步骤操作（注：此解题方法共有三步。由于本题不难，只用两步即可得出正确选项。三步完整的解题顺序见练习三第三题）：

解题第一步：主从句的逻辑关系要与原文一致。

原文：..., even though...(让步转折关系)，只有选项(A) Even though..., ...和选项(C) Although..., ...存在让步转折关系，所以将选项(B)(D)排除。

解题第二步：主句主干尽量与原文一致。

原文中的主句主干为：the structure of backbone shows that...

选项(A)主句主干为：it did not have a backbone，与原文主句主干不符，故错误。

选项(C)主句主干为：its backbone structure shows that...，与原文主句主干相同，故为正确选项。

11

PROPULSION

Propulsion is the power that moves something in a forward direction.

同义词：impetus, impulse, push

STAYING AFLOAT

If something or someone is **staying afloat** in a liquid, they are in the liquid, on or just below surface, and are being supported by it.

同义词: being buoyant, hovering, hanging

DIRECTION（→ CHANGING DIRECTION）

A **direction** is the general line that someone or something is moving or pointing in.

WEIGH（→ DECREASING WEIGHT）

If someone or something **weighs** a particular amount, this amount is how heavy they are.

MOVING FORWARD

If you **move** or look **forward**, you move or look in direction that is in front of you.

通过上面五个单词或词组的意义对比，可以得出与propulsion意义最相近的是选项(D) moving forward。

12

This is **a question** that...

在插入的句子中含有this/these/such之类的指示代词时，其解题方法为：■的前句话必须包含或符合这些词后面的名词的意义。若不满足这个条件，则■的位置必错。

因此，“这是一个……问题”要放入到原文中，■的前句话应该是一个问题。而满足这个条件的只有第二个位置的■。故选第二个位置。

13

提示句：This passage discusses fossils that help to explain the likely origins of cetaceans—whales, porpoises, and dolphins.

(1)	✔	第一段的主旨内容。
(2)	✔	第五段的主旨内容。
(3)	✘	本句话为第四段的细节信息，并不是文章的主要观点。
(4)	✘	第三段的细节信息，它在文章中不是被主要论述的观点。
(5)	✔	第一段的主旨内容。
(6)	✘	第五段的细节信息。

结构题的解题方法总论

1. 错误选项特征

i 未被原文提及的内容为错

ii 与原文观点相反的内容为错

iii 原文中的minor ideas为错

minor ideas（次要观点）与most important ideas（重要观点）的区别

most important ideas在原文中处于被支持、被说明的地位；minor ideas在文章中只是起到支持、说明most important ideas的作用，而minor ideas的成立不需要其他观点支持。

判断minor ideas的方法：minor ideas在原文中没有论述的必要性。另外，事实性叙述内容、定义式内容多为minor ideas，具体的数字性内容必为minor ideas。

2. 正确选项特征

i 段落核心内容（常为段首句）

ii 正确选项必须与提示句的主旨相关

提示句：同本题所给出的提示原文主旨的句子（the introductory sentence for a brief summary of the passage provided by the text）。

本文词汇总结

adaptation	*n.*	适应，适应性变化
affinity	*n.*	亲缘关系；密切关系
cetacean	*n.*	鲸类动物，鲸鱼
conceal	*v.*	隐藏，隐瞒
disguise	*v.*	隐瞒，掩饰；伪装
embedded	*adj.*	嵌入的，插入的
envision	*v.*	想象；预见
functional	*adj.*	有功能的，起作用的
gill	*n.*	鳃
intermediate	*adj.*	中间的；居间的
locomotion	*n.*	运动；移动
marine	*adj.*	海洋的，海的
propulsion	*n.*	推进；推进力
rear	*adj.*	后面的，背面的
retain	*v.*	保留
streamlined	*adj.*	流线型的

Practice Set 2
DESERT FORMATION

文章结构

标 题	沙漠化
第一段	沙漠已经占据了地球陆地面积的四分之一，而又有四分之一的陆地也面临着沙漠化的威胁。
第二段	沙漠化的主要成因是地表植被的破坏，导致土壤被风或水带走。
第三段	植被的破坏导致土壤蓄水能力的下降，进而又导致植被的减少，最终地表不断退化。
第四段	全球气候的持续变暖加剧了一些地区的干旱状态，进而使沙漠化程度加重。
第五段	在大部分地区，人类活动而非自然环境是造成沙漠化的主要因素。
第六段	导致沙漠化的四种人类活动之一：过度耕作。
第七段	导致沙漠化的四种人类活动之一：过度放牧。
第八段	导致沙漠化的四种人类活动之一：薪柴的获取和对动物粪便的利用。
第九段	导致沙漠化的四种人类活动之一：过度灌溉。
第十段	沙漠化的影响是长久的，被破坏的土壤需要几百年甚至几千年才能恢复。

题目解析

1

<u>**THREATEN**</u>

If something or someone **threatens** a person or thing, they are likely to harm that person or thing.

同义词: endanger, imperil, jeopardize, put at risk

RESTRICT

If you **restrict** something, you put a limit on it in order to reduce it or prevent it becoming too great.

同义词: hamper, impede, confine, restrain

ENDANGER

To **endanger** something or someone means to put them in a situation where they might be harmed or destroyed completely.

同义词: threaten, imperil, risk, jeopardize, put at risk, put in danger

PREVENT

To **prevent** something means to ensure that it does not happen.

同义词: avoid, hamper, hinder, impede, inhibit, frustrate

REJECT

If you **reject** something such as proposal, a request, or an offer, you do not accept it or you do not agree to it.

同义词: deny, decline, exclude, veto

通过上面五个单词的意义对比，可以得出与threatened意义最接近的是选项(B) endangered。

2

关键词：the loss of natural vegetation, consequences for soil

定位句：Even in the areas that retain a soil cover, the reduction of vegetation typically results in the loss of the soil's ability to absorb substantial quantities of water.

解题方法：直选法

(B) reduced water absorption

此选项是原文定位句的同义转述，必然是细节题的正确答案。

3

DELICATE

If something is **delicate**, it is easy to harm, damage, or break, and needs to be handled or treated carefully.

同义词: fragile, tender, weak

FRAGILE

Something that is **fragile** is easily broken or damaged.

同义词: delicate, brittle, weak, breakable, flimsy

PREDICTABLE

If you say that an event is **predictable**, you mean that it is obvious in advance that it will happen.

同义词: likely, anticipated, expected, foreseeable

COMPLEX

Something that is **complex** has many different parts, and is therefore often difficult to understand.

同义词: complicated, sophisticated, intricate

VALUABLE

见练习一第三题词汇题解析。

通过上面五个单词的意义对比，可以得出与delicate意义最接近的是选项(A) fragile。

另外，大家还需要记住：

【考】delicate = dainty

【英】attractive because of being soft, gentle, light, etc.; pleasant or attractive in a way that is not too strong

【汉】*adj.*（颜色）柔和的，（味道）清淡可口的

【预】subtle, tender, fine

【例】They enjoyed the **delicate** flavor of the wine.

【考】delicate = elegant

【英】easily torn or damaged; fragile

【汉】*adj.* 精致的，精美的

【预】fine, deft, graceful, skilled, subtle

【例】The fabric has a **delicate** floral print.

4

关键词：in dry periods, border areas

定位句：During the dry periods that are common phenomena along the desert margins, though, the pressure on the land is often far in excess of its diminished capacity, and desertification results.

解题方法：排除法

(B) retaining ~~their fertility after~~ desertification

此选项必错。

思路1：因为retaining their fertility是原文定位句中未出现过的信息，而涉及原文定位句以外的信息的选项是错误的。（详细讲解见练习一第七题“选项陷阱”）

简捷思路：看到该选项中有fertility，而原文定位句并未涉及，直接判断此选项为错。

思路2：根据原文，是因为“对土地的压力远远超过了土地可以承受的能力，才导致了沙漠化”，而这个选项中的after desertification告诉我们，它是在讲沙漠化之后的情况，而关于沙漠化之后情况是怎么样的，原文定位句并没有说明。所以，从这个角度来讲，该选项也是错误的。

简捷思路：看到该选项中有after，而原文定位句中并不是讲desertification之后的情况，所以判断此选项错误。

(C) providing water for ~~irrigating crops~~

irrigating crops在原文的定位句中并没有涉及，所以该选项错误。

(D) ~~attracting populations~~ in search of food and fuel

attracting populations在原文的定位句中并没有涉及，所以该选项错误。

所以，此题正确选项为(A) adjusting to stresses created by settlement，其中stresses就是原文定位句pressure的同义替代词。原文说 “在沙漠边界地区的干旱时期，由于对土地的压力远远大于了它能够承受的能力，所以导致沙漠化”，这也就说明，土地在调节自己适应这种压力（adjusting to stresses）的方面出现了问题。

总结：这道题稍有难度。在做题时，能通过原文的意思直接选出(A)为正确答案的概率较小。因此，在无法用直选法有根据地判断出哪个选项必然正确时，可以用排除法。本题中，通过(B) (C) (D)三个选项的共同特征——都涉及了原文定位句以外的信息，将此三个选项排除。

5

PROGRESSIVE（→ PROGRESSIVELY）

A **progressive** change happens gradually over a period of time.

同义词: increasing, advancing, growing, developing, ongoing

OPEN（→ OPENLY）

If you describe a situation, attitude, or way of behaving as **open**, you mean it is not kept hidden or secret.

同义词: unrestricted, unoccupied, accessible, available

IMPRESSIVE（→ IMPRESSIVELY）

Something that is **impressive** impresses you, for example because it is great in size or degree, or is done with a great deal of skill.

同义词: grand, awesome, striking, dramatic

OBJECTIVE（→ OBJECTIVELY）

① **Objective** information is based on facts.

② If someone is **objective**, they base their opinions on facts rather than on their personal feelings.

同义词: unbiased, detached, impartial, unprejudiced

INCREASE(→ INCREASINGLY)

If something **increases** or you **increase** it, it becomes greater in number, level, or amount.

同义词: grow, advance, boost, develop, expand, extend, enlarge

通过上面五个单词的意义对比，可以得出与progressively意义最接近的是选项(D) increasingly。

6

关键词：raising crops

定位句：Since the raising of most crops necessitates the prior removal of the natural vegetation, ...

解题方法：直选法

(C) Removal of the original vegetation

此选项是原文定位句的同义转述，是细节题的正确答案。

7

DEVOID OF

If you say that someone or something is **devoid of** a quality of thing, you are emphasizing that they have none of it.

同义词: lacking, deficient, empty, free from

CONSIST OF（→ CONSISTING OF）

Something that **consists of** particular things or people is formed from them.

同义词: be composed of, comprise, contain, include, involve

HIDDEN BY

① **Hidden** facts, feelings, activities, or problems are not easy to notice or discover.

② A **hidden** place is difficult to find.

同义词: concealed, latent, unseen, secret

EXCEPT FOR

You use **except for** to introduce the only thing or person that prevents a statement from being completely true.

LACKING IN

① If you say that someone or something **lacks** a particular quality or that a particular quality is **lacking in** them, you mean that they do not have any or enough of it.

同义词: be short of, be without

通过上面五组词的意义对比，可以得出与devoid of意义最接近的是选项(D) lacking in。

8

关键词：excess water, desertification

定位句：Excess water from irrigation sinks down into the water table. If no drainage system exists, the water table rises, bringing dissolved salts to the surface.

解题方法：直选法

(D) bring salts to the surface

此选项是原文定位句的重复叙述，符合细节题正确选项的待征。

错误选项讲解：

(B) ~~limit~~ the evaporation of water

原文确实提过 "The water evaporates...," 但只是说 "水蒸发了" ，并没有 "限制（limit）" 水的蒸发。所以，该选项涉及原文定位句中未提及的内容，为错误选项。

(C) require ~~more~~ absorption of air by the soil

这个选项很多考生都会误选。原文为 "...a white crustal layer that prevents air and water from reaching the underlying soil" ，这句话只是说 "白色的盐层妨碍了空气和水到达它们下

面的土壤”，但并不表示“土壤因此需要吸收更多的（more）空气”。这并不是原文所表达的意思，所以该选项仍然错误。

注意：选项(C)的错误很有代表性。大家可以记住这个判断标准：原文中没有比较级或最高级，答案中也不可以出现；出现比较级或最高级的选项在多数情况下是错误的。

思路关联

练习三第一题，练习六第六题选项(B)

9

本题的正确选项属于第二种类型：

(C) insufficient irrigation

该选项与第九段首句The final major human cause of desertification is soil salinization resulting from over-irrigation的意思完全相反，所以为本题的正确答案。

NOT/ EXCEPT题型

以下两种选项经常是该题型的正确答案：

Ⅰ 原文未提及的选项

Ⅱ 与原文观点相反、相矛盾的选项

10

句子简化题

此题的考点：“并列结构”（and = as well as)

并列结构

在并列连词（and, as well as）之后若出现介词(in, for, of, to...)，则应找在并列连词前面出现这些相同介词的地方，后一个介词与前面的相同介词共用其之前的一切成分；若在并列连词之后出现动词或分词，则应找在并列连词之前出现的与其词性相同的词，并与其共用之前的一切成分。

此题结构：...results from..., as well as from...，即：...results from..., as well as results from...，由于results from = because，所以本题等同于...because..., as well as because...。

选项(A)中主从句逻辑关系与原文结构相同，且其主干内容与原文一致。因此为本题的正确答案。

原 文		选 项
The extreme seriousness of desertification	=	Desertification is a significant problem
results from the vast areas of land and tremendous numbers of people affected	=	affects large areas of land and great numbers of people
as well as from the great difficulty of reversing or even slowing the process	=	because it is so hard to reverse

11

推论题：只针对原文提及的内容进行推论，涉及其他方面的选项均错。

解题方法：排除法

(A) ~~Governments~~ will act quickly to control further desertification.

(B) The factors influencing desertification ~~occur in cycles~~ and ~~will change~~ in the future.

(D) Desertification ~~will soon occur in all areas~~ of the world.

此三个选项中被划删除线的内容均是原文未曾涉及的信息。故全为错。

12

本句中含有“this...”这个结构，此结构的解题思路见练习一第12题中的具体讲解。“This economic reliance on livestock in certain regions”这个概念必须在■的前句话被提及。所以第一个■位置为错。第二个■的前句话“the raising of livestock is a major economic activity in semiarid lands,...”是对“economic reliance on livestock in certain regions”这个意思的同义表达。所以第二个■位置正确。

13

提示句：Many factors have contributed to the great increase in desertification in recent decades.

(1)	✔	第六段总体讲完四个factors后，主要讲解了第一个因素over-cultivation。
(2)	✘	本文重点讲导致沙漠化的人为因素。此选项说庄稼的成活率降低，与本文主旨无关。
(3)	✔	第七、八段的主旨内容为over-grazing and firewood gathering。
(4)	✔	第九段的主旨内容为over-irrigation。
(5)	✘	角度1：事实性内容为原文的minor idea。 角度2：本题考查造成沙漠化的因素，而本选项的内容为"动物粪便能肥沃土壤"，显然这并不是造成沙漠化的因素，故排除。
(6)	✘	事实性内容为原文的minor idea。

本文词汇总结

aridity	*n.*	干旱；荒芜
conditioner	*n.*	调节剂；调节器
density	*n.*	密度；稠密
desertification	*n.*	沙漠化
deterioration	*n.*	退化；恶化；变坏
diminished	*adj.*	减少了的
dominant	*adj.*	统治的；占优势的
drainage	*n.*	排水，排水装置
excess	*n.*	超出，过量
expand	*v.*	扩展，扩张
grazing	*n.*	放牧
identify	*v.*	确认；鉴别，识别
irrigation	*n.*	灌溉
penetration	*n.*	渗透，渗入

previously	*adv.*	以前，先前
primarily	*adv.*	主要地
prior	*adj.*	在前的，在先的
pulverization	*n.*	粉碎，粉化
salinization	*n.*	盐碱渍化
substantial	*adj.*	很多的，大量的
substitute	*n.*	代替品，代用品
susceptible	*adj.*	易受影响的
trample	*v.*	踩踏，践踏

Practice Set 3
EARLY CINEMA

文章结构

标 题	早期电影
第一段	早期电影形式是小孔放映（即西洋镜或拉洋片）。
第二段	早期的活动电影放映室采取的是留声机放映室的形式。
第三段	为了追求利润最大化，放映者在第一间活动电影放映室问世一年后便优化了放映设备。
第四段	随着投影技术的出现，电影成为大众消费的最终形式。
第五段	由于电影自身的特点和观众所关注的重点，早期放映者对电影放映的方式所能起到的作用是有限的。
第六段	随着投影技术的出现，观众与影片的关系变得公开化。

题目解析

1

NOT/ EXCEPT题型：具体解法见练习二第九题。

解题思路1：

采用NOT/EXCEPT题型解题方法Ⅰ。由于(A) (B) (D) 三个选项在原文中均被明确提及，故选项(C) 为正确答案。

定位句：..., which contained only a few individual machines and permitted only one customer to view a short, 50-foot film at one time. [(A) (D) 选项出处]

The first Kinetoscope parlors contained five machines. For the price of 25 cents (or 5 cents per machine), customers moved from machine to machine to watch five different films. [(B)选项出处]

解题思路2：

定位句：in the case of famous prizefights, successive rounds of a single fight。

练习二第八题中曾经提到的一种错误选项的辨别思路：若原文中没有出现比较级或最高级，而选项中出现了，一般为错。本题选项(C) Prizefights were the most popular subjects for films，而原文定位句中只说明prizefights是famous，并不是the most popular subjects，符合错误选项的特征。本题为NOT/EXCEPT题型，这种题型的正确选项应该是相对其他题型而言的错误选项，所以在本题中选项(C)为正确答案。

修辞目的题型

这种题型一般的考法是问文章为什么要提到某个词或某个句子（discusses...in order to...），而考查的词或句子多数情况下会在原文用阴影显示。

解法：先读考点（考查的词或句子）所在的句子，再读它的前句或后句，总结这两句话的关系即可。

2

关键词：phonograph parlors

定位句：These Kinetoscope arcades were modeled on phonograph parlors, which had proven successful for Edison several years earlier.

译文：这些Kinetoscope arcades是通过模仿phonograph parlors而制造出来的，几年前爱迪生已经证明phonograph parlors是成功的。

解题方法：直选法

(B) describe the model used to design Kinetoscope parlors

可见，提到phonograph parlors的目的是为了说明Kinetoscope arcades的制作原理，即选项(B)。

3

本题中含有明确的逻辑关系词，故采取以下步骤解题。

解题第一步：主从句的逻辑关系要与原文一致。

原文：..., reasoning that (=because)...(因果关系)，只有选项(B) ...because...和选项(C) ...because...符合因果关系，所以将选项(A)(D)排除。

解题第二步：主句主干尽量与原文一致。

原文中的主句主干为：He refused to develop projection technology

选项(B)主句主干为：Edison refused to work on projection technology，与原文主句主干相符，故保留。

选项(C)主句主干为：Edison did not want to develop projection technology，与原文主句主干相同，故保留。

解题第三步：从句主干尽量与原文一致。

原文中的从句主干为：..., then exhibitors would purchase only one machine—a projector—from him instead of several.

选项(B)中的从句主干为：he did not think exhibitors would replace their projectors with newer machines，与原文从句主干意思不符，故错误。

选项(C)中的从句主干为：it limited the number of machines he could sell，与原文从句意思一致，故为正确答案。

4

READILY

You use **readily** to say that something can be done or obtained quickly and easily. For example, if you say that something can be readily understood, you mean that people can understand it quickly and easily.

同义词: easily, quickly, smoothly, speedily, effortlessly

FREQUENT（→ FREQUENTLY）

If something is **frequent**, it happens often.

同义词: often, common, repeated

EASILY

You use **easily** to say that something happens more quickly or more often than is usual or normal.

同义词: readily, with ease, smoothly, without difficulty

INTELLIGENT（→ INTELLIGENTLY）

A person or animal that is **intelligent** has the ability to think, understand, and learn things quickly and well.

同义词: clever, bright, smart, enlightened

OBVIOUSLY

You use **obviously** to indicate that something is easily noticed, seen or recognized.

同义词: clearly, manifestly, unquestionably, without doubt

通过上面五个单词的意义对比，可以得出与readily意义相近的是选项(B) easily。

5

ASSISTANCE

If you give someone **assistance**, you help them do a job or task by doing part of the work.

同义词: help, aid, cooperation, support, backing

CRITICISM

① **Criticism** is the action of expressing disapproval of something or someone.

② A **criticism** is a statement that expresses disapproval.

同义词: disapproval, fault-finding

LEADERSHIP

You refer to people who are in control of a group or organization as the **leadership**.

同义词: domination, management, direction, guidance

HELP

If you **help** someone, you make it easier for them to do something, for example by doing part of the work for them or by giving them advice or money.

同义词: assistance, aid, cooperation, support

APPROVAL

Approval is a formal or official statement that something is acceptable.

同义词: permission, consent, assent

通过上面五个单词的意义对比，可以得出与assistance意义接近的是选项(C) help。

6

关键词：movies differ from previous spectacles

定位句：But the movies differed significantly from these other forms of entertainment①, which depended on either live performance or (in the case of the slide-and-lantern shows) ② the active involvement of a master of ceremonies who assembled the final program.

解题方法：直选法

(D) They did not require live entertainers.

本题采用"取非"的解题思路（详细阐述见练习一第二题）

定位句中，which引导的定语从句修饰these other forms of entertainment, 而前面指明movies与these other forms of entertainment不同，所以应该把这个定语从句的内容取非。

① these other forms of entertainment: these + n. 结构，该n.（名词）或其同义词在前文应该被提及，否则该句话无意义。在原文中，这句话的前句话为Previously, large audiences had viewed spectacles at the theater, where...，所以these other forms of entertainment在这里应该指代spectacles viewed by large audiences，即本题的关键词。

②括号内的内容可以略过不读。

7

关键词：early exhibitors, presentation of movies, theaters

定位句：Although early exhibitors regularly accompanied movies with live acts,... Even though early exhibitors shaped their film programs by mixing films and other entertainments together...

解题方法1：直选法

(A) They decided how to combine various components of the film program.

这个选项中的combine与原文定位句中的accompanied...with...和mixing...and...所表达的意思相同，按照细节题正确答案的特征：与原文定位句是同义转述关系的选项（常体现为同义词的替代）为正确答案，所以即可判断此题选项(A)正确。但是，从这个角度做此题有些难度。要看出本题中答案与原文的这种同义转述关系，需要大家对词义对应非常敏感，正如对练习一第一题选项(C)和练习六第三题选项(D)的判断一样。由于这种思路的养成需要多加练习，但在做本题时，很多人可能考虑不到这种解题思路，所以下面给大家提供本题的第二种解题方法：排除法。

解题方法2：排除法

(B) They ~~advised filmmakers~~ on appropriate movie content.

(C) They often ~~took part in~~ the live-action performances.

这两个选项比较容易判断，划删除线的部分都是原文未曾提及的内容，符合细节题错误选项的特征，故可以直接排除。具体内容见练习一第七题“错误选项讲解”。

(D) They produced and prerecorded the material that was shown in the theaters.

这个选项为“混淆选项”，在解题时很容易被误选。“混淆选项”永远为错误答案。其特征如下：

混淆选项特征

原文给出逻辑关系为：A → B, C → D

选项中的逻辑关系为：A → D

这个选项迷惑之处在于原文确实提过A、D这两个事物，如果考生凭印象做题，就容易认为这个选项的内容是之前读到过的，应该是正确信息，从而选择这个答案。但需要注意的是，选项中A、D两事物之间的逻辑关系在原文中并没有被表述，因此是错误选项。

在本题中，原文定位句为：the substance of the movies themselves is mass-produced, prerecorded material that can easily be reproduced by theaters with little or no active participation by the exhibitor. 也就是说，这些material是由theaters制造的，并不是early exhibitors。而选项（D）中的they指代early exhibitors。故该选项错误。

8

关键词：Mutoscope differed from the Kinetoscope

定位句：With the advent of projection, the viewer's relationship with the image was no longer private, as it had been with earlier peepshow devices such as the Kinetoscope and the Mutoscope, which was a similar machine that reproduced motion by means of successive images on individual photographic cards instead of on strips of celluloid.

译文：……早期的peepshow devices，比如说Kinetoscope和Mutoscope。Mutoscope是一台与Kinetoscope比较相似的机器，它是用photographic cards上面的连续影像而不是用strips of celluloid来制造电影的。（这里暗指，Kinetoscope是用strips of celluloid制造电影。）

解题方法：直选法

(D) A different type of material was used to produce the images used in the Mutoscope.

本题的考点在原文定位句中的两个从句。

9

指代题

正确选项：(B) the viewer's relationship with the image

本题只是考查了一个简单的意义重复：

With the advent of projection, the viewer's relationship with the image was no longer private, ...It suddenly became public...

no longer private = public，即 it 这句话是在重复上一句话的意思，所以it = the viewer's relationship with the image。

10

关键词：images seen by viewers, in the earlier peepshows, on the screen

定位句：At the same time, the image that the spectator looked at expanded from the minuscule peepshow dimensions of 1 or 2 inches (in height) to the life-size proportions of 6 or 9 feet.

解题方法：直选法

(A) small in size

数字考点

在托福阅读文章中经常会出现数字，而这些数字所在的句子往往会成为考点，考查这些数字在文章说明了什么问题。通常有以下两种情况：

1. 若文章中出现单独的数字，这个数字本身并不能说明任何问题，它是为了支持前面的内容而存在的。所以，要弄清楚这个数字说明的问题，应该再读它前面的内容。

比如，在“我用了3千美元买一幅画”这句话中，数字“3千”不能说明任何问题，既不能表明某人是用很多钱买了这幅画，也不能表明某人是用较少的钱买了这幅画。要选出正确答案（也就是这个数字所说明的问题），需要再读它前面的内容，看前面的观点是表示用钱多，还是用钱少。

2. 若文章中有多个数字同时出现，则这些数字之间的比较即成为考点。

例如：“我用3千美元买了一幅画，而他用3百美元也买了一幅相同的画。”这可以直接比较得出结论：我买这幅画用的钱多，他买这幅画用的钱少。

而本题为数字考点的第二种情况，直接将“1 or 2 inches”与“6 or 9 feet”作比较，可得出the images in the earlier peepshows compared with the images projected on the screen are small in size，即选项(A)。

思路关联：练习六第十题考点与本题相同。

11

EXPAND

If something **expands** or is expanded, it becomes larger.

同义词: enlarge, extend, increase, broaden, magnify, amplify

ENLARGE

When you **enlarge** something or when it enlarges, it becomes bigger.

同义词: expand, extend, amplify, grow, increase, add to, broaden

IMPROVE

If something **improves** or if you improve it, it gets better.

同义词: enhance, advance, upgrade

VARY

If something varies or if you **vary** it, it becomes different or changed.

同义词: change, diversify

REJECT

If you **reject** something such as a proposal, a request, or an offer, you do not accept it or you do not agree to it.

同义词: deny, decline, disallow, exclude, renounce, veto, refuse, turn down

通过上面五个单词的意义对比，可以得出与expanded意义最接近的是选项(A) was enlarged。

12

本句中含有"this..."这个结构，此结构的解题思路请见练习一第12题中的具体讲解。

This widespread use of projection technology 这个概念必须在■的前句话被提及。在本题中，第四个■的前句话：these early projection devices were used in...是对widespread use of projection technology这个意思的同义表达。所以第四个■位置正确。

句子插入题补充说明

1. 位于段首位置的■多数情况下为错。

因为段首句通常为段落的主旨内容，它不是一句可有可无的话。而对于句子插入题而言，要放入原文的句子在原文中是一句可有可无的话，也就是说有没有它的存在都不会改变原文的逻辑关系。因此对于本题而言，第一个■位置就先不需要考虑了。

2. 如果■后面的句子里出现代词，这个■位置也暂不需要考虑。

因为如果在这个■位置放入一句话，则很有可能改变它后面句子中代词的指代对象，从而改变了那句话在原文中的意思。而我们刚刚在第一点中说过，插入之后的句子不能改变原文原有的逻辑关系，所以这样的■位置一般情况下是错误的。在本题中第三个■位置的后一句话中有these early projection devices这种“指示代词＋名词”的形式，指代前文的内容，因此这个位置的■在做题时暂不考虑。

13

提示句：The technology for modern cinema evolved at the end of the nineteenth century.

(1)	✘	事实性内容为细节内容，不是全文论述的中心。
(2)	✘	文章未提及的内容。
(3)	✔	第一、二段论述内容。
(4)	✘	与提示句的主旨信息无关，必错。
(5)	✔	第六段主要论述内容。
(6)	✔	第一、六段论述内容。

本文词汇总结

admission	*n.*	入场费
accompany	*v.*	给…附加
consumption	*n.*	消费
manipulation	*n.*	操作，控制，处理
marvel	*n.*	令人惊奇的事物
model	*v.*	模仿；以…为模型
participation	*n.*	参加，参与
project	*v.*	放映
spectacle	*n.*	表演，演出
spectator	*n.*	观众
ultimate	*adj.*	最后的，终极的

Practice Set 4
AGGRESSION

文章结构

标 题	侵略性
第一段	心理学家采用多种方式来理解人类的侵略性行为。
第二段	生物学研究方法：许多生物结构和体内激素引发侵略行为。
第三段	生物社会学的观点认为，侵略性是自然选择的结果，是遗传的。
第四段	生物社会学的观点受到多方质疑。
第五段	心理动力学研究方法：内心的冲突是造成人类侵略行为的主要原因。
第六段	心理动力学的观点认为，避免侵略性行为的最佳方法是寻找情绪和压力的纾解渠道。
第七段	认知学研究方法：人类的行为是由价值观决定的。
第八段	认知学的观点认为，不愉快的情绪诱发侵略性行为，但不是自发的，而是有认知性因素的介入。

题目解析

1

关键词：aggression in animals, hypothalamus

定位句：One is the hypothalamus, a region of the brain. In response to certain stimuli, many animals show instinctive aggressive reactions. The hypothalamus appears to be involved in this inborn reaction pattern: electrical stimulation of part of the hypothalamus triggers stereotypical aggressive behaviors in many animals.

解题方法：排除法

(A) Some aggressive animal species have a ~~highly developed~~ hypothalamus.

(B) Electrical stimulation of the hypothalamus ~~delays animals' inborn reaction patterns~~.

(D) Animals who ~~lack a hypothalamus~~ display few aggressive tendencies.

以上三个选项中划删除线部分均为原文未提及的内容。

可见，由排除法得出本题正确答案为选项(C)。

2

关键词：Darwin's theory of evolution, members of a species, struggle for survival

定位句：Consider Darwin's theory of evolution. Darwin held that many more individuals are produced than can find food and survive into adulthood. A struggle for survival follows.

解题方法：直选法

(C) many more individuals are born than can survive until the age of reproduction

同义替代关系如下：

原文		选项
many more individuals are produced	=	many more individuals are born
can find food and survive	=	can survive
adulthood	=	the age of reproduction

3

INEVITABLE

If something is **inevitable**, it is certain to happen and cannot be prevented or avoided.

同义词: unavoidable, assured, certain, destined, fixed

UNAVOIDABLE

If something is **unavoidable**, it cannot be avoided or prevented.

同义词: inevitable, certain, fated

REGRETTABLE

You describe something as **regrettabl**e when you think that it is bad and that it should not happen or have happened.

同义词: unfortunate, disappointing, distressing, lamentable

CONTROLLABLE

If something is **controllable** you are able to control or influence it.

UNSUITABLE

Someone or something that is **unsuitable** for a particular purpose or situation does not have the right qualities for it.

同义词: inappropriate, improper, unfitting, inapt

通过上面五个单词的意义对比，可以得出与inevitable意义最接近的是选项(A) unavoidable。

另外，大家还需要记住：

【考】inevitable = without exception

【英】sure to happen

【汉】*adj.* 不可避免的

【预】certain, fixed, sure

【例】Some criticism was **inevitable**.

4

GRATIFY

If you **gratify** your own or another person's desire, you do what is necessary to please yourself or them.

同义词: satisfy, please, delight

IDENTIFY

见练习一第六题解析。

MODIFY

If you **modify** something, you change it slightly, usually in order to improve it.

同义词: adjust, alter, convert, remodel, revise, change

SATISFY

If someone or something **satisfies** you, they give you enough of what you want or need to make you pleased or contented.

同义词: gratify, content, lease, indulge

SIMPLIFY

If you **simplify** something, you make it easier to understand or you remove the things that make it complex.

同义词: abridge, streamline

通过上面五个单词的意义对比，可以得出与gratify意义最接近的是选项(C) satisfy。

5

指代题

考点：代词的连续指代关系

定位句：Pent-up aggressive impulses demand outlets. They may be expressed toward..., or they may be expressed toward...

正确选项：(B) pent-up aggressive impulses

6

关键词：Freud, children, a desire to vent aggression on their parents

定位句：Sigmund Freud, for example, believed that aggressive impulses are inevitable reactions to the frustrations of daily life. Children normally desire to vent aggressive impulses on other people, including their parents, because even the most attentive parents cannot gratify all of their demands immediately. Yet children, also fearing their parents' punishment and the loss of parental love, come to repress most aggressive impulses.

解题方法：直选法

(B) a fear that their parents will punish them and stop loving them

该选项与原文定位句是同义替代关系，必为正确答案。

原 文		选 项
fearing	=	a fear
their parents' punishment	=	their parents will punish them
the loss of parental love	=	stop loving them

7

关键词：steam engines

定位句：The Freudian perspective, in a sense, sees us as "steam engines." By holding in rather than venting "steam," we set the stage for future explosions. Pent-up aggressive impulses demand outlets. They may be expressed toward parents in indirect ways such as destroying furniture, or they may be expressed toward strangers later in life.

解题方法：直选法

(C) must vent their aggression to prevent it from building up

原文定位句中的下划线部分是对前面“steam engines”的解释，该选项与原文定位句下划线部分意义相同，故正确。

8

原文层次划分：

People [who believe that aggression is necessary and justified—as during wartime—] are likely to act aggressively, whereas people [who believe that a particular war or act of aggression is unjust, or who think that aggression is never justified,] are less likely to behave aggressively.

“[ ]”中的内容为两个定语从句，修饰各自前面的people。该句的主要部分为：people are likely to act aggressively, whereas people are less likely to behave aggressively.

正确答案为选项(B)，与原文关系一致。

选项(A)极容易被误选。它的错误之处在于：原文说“……的人有可能(likely)有暴力行为，……的人发生暴力行为的可能性会小些（less likely)”。但选项(A)将原文中的“likely”丢失，就变成了“……的人会发生暴力行为，……的人不会发生暴力行为”，把原文中的“可能性”变成了“必然性”，严重改变了原文的句义，故错误。

9

NOT/ EXCEPT 题型：

本题采用第一种解题方法

(C) instinct to avoid aggression

其余三个选项均被原文提及。

定位句：**The Cognitive Approach**. Cognitive psychologists assert that our behavior is influenced <u>by our values</u> [选项(A)出处], by the ways in which we interpret our situations, and by choice.

One cognitive theory suggests that aggravating and painful events trigger unpleasant feelings. ...People *decide* whether they will act aggressively or not on the basis of factors such as their experiences with aggression [选项(B)出处] and their interpretation of other people's motives [选项(D)出处].

10

DISTORT

If you **distort** a statement, fact, or idea, you report or represent it in an untrue way.

同义词: misrepresent, bias, twist

MISTRUST

If you **mistrust** someone or something, you do not trust them.

同义词: distrust, doubt, be wary of

MISINTERPRET

If you **misinterpret** something, you understand it wrongly.

同义词: distort, misunderstand, misrepresent, misjudge

CRITICIZE

If you **criticize** someone or something, you express your disapproval of them by saying what you think is wrong with them.

同义词: carp, censure, condemn

RESENT

If you **resent** someone or something, you feel bitter and angry about them.

同义词: be bitter about, grudge

通过上面五个单词的意义对比，可以得出与distort意义最接近的是选项(B) misinterpret。

另外，大家还需要记住：

【考】distort = deform

【英】to twist out of a natural, normal, or original shape or condition

【汉】*v.* 扭曲，变形

【预】bend, disfigure, misshape, twist

【例】The odd camera angle **distorted** her figure in the photograph.

11

According to Freud, however, impulses that have been repressed continue to exist and demand expression.

此句中“however”这个关联词表明，■前句话与本句之间是一种转折关系。

第二个■位置的前句话为“children...come to repress most aggressive impulses”（孩子们压抑了大部分侵略性冲动）与本句话（这种侵略性的冲动仍然存在，并且需要被发泄出来）之间正好是转折关系。故本题答案为第二个■位置。

12

此类题型考查细节定位能力：

Approach to Understanding Aggression	Associated Claims
Biological Approach	(2) 原文第三段第五行信息：A struggle for survival follows.
Psychodynamic Approach	(1) 原文第五段第十行信息：They maybe expressed toward parents in indirect ways such as destroying furniture, or they may be expressed toward strangers later in life. (6) 原文第五段第一行及第十行信息：Theorists adopting the psychodynamic approach hold that inner conflicts are crucial for understanding human behavior, including aggression. // Pent-up aggressive impulses demand outlets.

Approach to Understanding Aggression	Associated Claims
Cognitive Approach	(3) 原文第八段第三行信息：People *decide* whether they will act aggressively or not on the basis of factors such as their experiences with aggression and their interpretation of other people's motives. (5) 原文第七段第一行信息：Cognitive psychologists assert that our behavior is influenced by our values, by the ways in which we interpret our situations, and by choice.

本文词汇总结

aggravating	*adj.*	加重的，恶化的
analogy	*n.*	类比
assert	*v.*	认为，宣称
conflict	*n.*	冲突
crucial	*adj.*	重要的
distort	*v.*	曲解，歪曲（事实）
engage	*v.*	参与；从事，着手
frustration	*n.*	挫折，失败
gratify	*v.*	满足
impulse	*v.*	冲动
inevitable	*adj.*	无法避免的
instinctive	*adj.*	本能的，天生的
interpret	*v.*	解释，说明
intervene	*v.*	干涉，介入
involve	*v.*	使卷入
justified	*adj.*	有道理的，合理的
moderate	*v.*	使缓和
motive	*n.*	动机，目的
offshoot	*n.*	分支，旁支
outwit	*v.*	以智取胜
pent-up	*adj.*	被压抑的
perspective	*n.*	观点，看法
possess	*v.*	拥有；占有
repress	*v.*	抑制，压抑
stereotypical	*adj.*	典型的
subsequent	*adj.*	后来的，接着发生的
tension	*n.*	紧张，压力
trigger	*v.*	激发，引发
valve	*n.*	情绪发泄方式；阀（门）
variation	*n.*	变化，改变
vent	*v.*	发泄

Practice Set 5
ARTISANS AND INDUSTRIALIZATION

文章结构

标 题	技工与工业化
第一段	1815年后，美国工业从家庭作坊逐渐转为制造工厂。
第二段	让习惯于家庭作坊式工作的劳动力适应工厂作业并不容易。
第三段	工厂生产的新特点。
第四段	早期工人对工厂作业的诸多不适应。
第五段	在这种新兴的经济秩序中，工人们成立了劳动联盟，以维护自身利益。
第六段	随着社会生产细分化和差异化的出现，财富集中到了少数人手中，工人们丧失了对他们自己生活的掌控权。

题目解析

1

关键词：articles manufactured before 1815

定位句：Before 1815 manufacturing in the United States had been done in homes or shops by skilled artisans. As master craftworkers, they imparted the knowledge of their trades to apprentices and journeymen. In addition, women often worked in their homes part-time, making finished articles from raw material supplied by merchant capitalists.

解题方法：排除法

(A) They were ~~primarily~~ produced by women.

程度副词的误用为错误选项的一个特征。

原文说“women often worked in their homes **part-time**,...”，part-time这个词说明articles并不是主要（primarily）由women来做的。所以该选项错误。

(B) They were generally produced in shops rather than homes.

该选项所表述的内容与原文第一句话的内容（Before 1815 manufacturing in the United States had been done in homes or shops by skilled artisans. ）相反，必错。

(D) They were produced mostly ~~in large cities with extensive transportation networks~~.

划删除线的内容是定位句以外的信息，不能作为正确答案。

所以，最终排除结果为选项(C)。

2

本题的考点在于考查平行并列关系。具体讲解见练习二第十题。

Apprentices were considered part of the family, and masters were responsible not only for... but also for... and for...

这三个“for”是平行并列的关系，共用responsible。

这句话可以翻译为：学徒被当做家庭成员，师傅不仅教给他们手艺，还给他们提供一些教育，并且监督他们的道德行为。

选项(B)可翻译为：师傅的责任远远超出了只是教给学徒手艺的范围。

这个选项并不是很好，因为它不是原文的同义转述，倒像是对原文句义的概括总结。但其余选项都严重改变了原文的句义，所以只能选这个选项。

3

DISRUPT

If someone or something **disrupts** an event, system, or process, they cause difficulties that prevent it from continuing or operating in a normal way.

同义词: disturb, confuse, upset, spoil, disorganize, interrupt, intrude

PROLONG

To **prolong** something means to make it last longer.

同义词: stretch, lengthen, perpetuate

ESTABLISH

If someone **establishes** something such as an organization, a type of activity, or a set of rules, they create it or introduce it in such a way that it is likely to last for a long time.

同义词: create, constitute, form, found, inaugurate, institute, set up

FOLLOW

An event, activity, or period of time that **follows** a particular thing happens or comes after that thing, at a later time.

同义词: come after, accompany

UPSET

If events **upset** something such as a procedure or a state of affairs, they cause it to go wrong.

同义词: disturb, disorder, disorganize, spoil

通过上面五个单词的意义对比，可以得出与disrupted意义最接近的是选项(D) upset。

另外，大家还需要记住：

【考】disruptive = disturbing

【英】causing (something) to be unable to continue in the normal way; interrupting the normal progress or activity of (something)

【汉】*adj.* 扰乱的，破坏的

【预】disorderly, distracting, troublesome, unsetting

【例】She has a **disruptive** influence on the other students.

4

修辞目的题：这种题常问"原文中为什么要提到某个词或某句话/提到某个词或某句话的目的是什么?"

解题方法：先读题干考查的内容在原文中所处的句子；再读其前面的句子，这句话的意思往往就是题干内容在原文中要说明的问题。

本题中，考点在原文中所处的句子为：One mill worker who finally quit complained revealingly about “obedience to the ding-dong of the bell—just as though we are so many living machines.” 前面的一句话为：The first generation to experience these changes did not adopt the new attitudes easily.（第一代经历这些变革的人们并不能很容易地适应这些新规则。）

可见，原文引用工人的话就是为了支持其前面的这个观点。因此，指明了这种支持关系的选项(A) support the idea that it was difficult for workers to adjust to working in factories是正确答案。

5

NOT/ EXCEPT 题型

本题采用第一种解题方法

(D) contact among workers who were not managers

其余三个选项均被原文提及。

With the loss of personal freedom [选项(A)出处] also came the loss of standing in the community [选项(B)出处]. Unlike artisan workshops in which apprentices worked closely with the masters supervising them, factories sharply separated workers from management [选项(C)出处].

6

MOMENTUM（→ GATHER SOME MOMENTUM）

If a process or movement gains **momentum**, it keeps developing or happening more quickly and keeps becoming less likely to stop.

同义词: propulsion, push, force, impetus

PROGRESS（→ MAKE PROGRESS）

Progress is the process of gradually improving or getting nearer to achieving or completing something.

同义词: development, advance, breakthrough, growth, improvement

ACTIVE （→ BECOME ACTIVE）

Someone who is **active** moves around a lot or does a lot of things.

同义词: busy, lively, vigorous, acting, at work

CHANGE （→ CAUSE CHANGES）

If there is a **change** in something, it becomes different.

同义词: alternation, innovation, mutation, transition

COMBINE （→ COMBINE FORCES）

If you **combine** two or more things or if they combine, they exist together.

同义词: join together, blend, integrate, merge, mix

通过上面五个单词的意义对比，可以得出与gathered some momentum意义最相近的是选项(A) made progress。

7

SPEARHEAD

If someone **spearheads** a campaign or an attack, they lead it.

同义词: lead, head, initiate, launch, pioneer, set off

LEAD

If you **lead** a group of people, an organization, or an activity, you are in control or in charge of the people or the activity.

同义词: direct, head, manage

ACCEPT

If you **accept** something that you have been offered, you say yes to it or agree to take it.

同义词: acquire, receive, obtain, agree to, admit, approve

CHANGE

见上题CAUSE CHANGES词条解析。

RESIST

If you **resist** something such as a change, you refuse to accept it and try to prevent it.

同义词: oppose, combat, hinder, defy, avoid

通过上面五个单词的意义对比，可以得出与spearheaded意义最接近的是选项(A) led。

8

关键词：labor movement of the 1800s

解题方法：排除法

(A) It was ~~successful~~ during times of economic crisis.

划删除线的部分为原文未提及的内容，由此可以直接排除此选项。并且，该选项也与原文所陈述的内容"..., but in the depression that followed, labor's strength collapsed"相反，仍为错误选项。

(B) Its ~~primary purpose~~ was to benefit unskilled labors.

(D) It helped workers of ~~all skill levels~~ form a ~~strong bond with each other~~.

在这两个选项中，划删除线部分均为原文未提及的内容，都可以直接排除。

所以选项(C) It was slow to improve conditions for workers. 为正确答案。

第五段的最后一句话"More than a decade of agitation did finally bring a workday shortened to 10 hours to most industries by the 1850s, and the courts also recognized workers' right to strike, but these gains had little immediate impact."与选项(C)所表述的内容基本相同，所以这也可以说明选项(C)为正确答案。但真正解题时，通过这种方式来直接判断正确答案有些困难，所以建议大家还是用排除法。

9

关键词：political party loyalties, and disagreements over tactics

定位句：Workers were united in resenting the industrial system and their loss of status, but they were divided by ethnic and racial antagonisms, gender, conflicting religious perspectives, occupational differences, political party loyalties, and disagreements over tactics.

解题方法：直选法

(B) created divisions among workers

原文指明：工人们因为ethnic and racial antagonisms, gender, conflicting religious perspectives, occupational differences, political party loyalties, and disagreements over tactics这些因素而彼此分离。所以，political party loyalties, and disagreements over tactics就是造成工人分离的两个因素。

10

固定解题思路

原文定位句为：	... x and/ or y...
关于该定位句的任何类型的题目：	________________?
选项设置：	(A) x (B) y (C) q (D) z

若某题符合上述特征，则该题的正确答案一定是在(C)和(D)选项中。(A)(B)两选项必错，不用考虑。

理由：在原文中，x、y用and/or连接，表达一种并列关系，也就是说在这样的结构中，选择其中任何一个作为正确选项时，都无法解释为什么不能选另外一个。所以，只能是这两个选项都不作为正确答案。

本题用此思路可以将(B)(C)两选项排除，它们在原文中是用“and”连接的。

选项(D)出现在该代词的后面。代词一般与它前面句子中的名词发生指代关系，且该选项代入原文后完全无法翻译，因而也可以将其排除。

故本题正确答案为(A) workers。

思路关联

练习六第二题。

11

本句中含有“this...”这个结构，此结构的解题思路请见练习一第12题中的具体讲解。

This new form of manufacturing 这个概念必须在■的前句话被提及。

本题解题思路1：

由于第三个■后的句子为：After 1815 this older form of manufacturing...，“this older form of manufacturing”意味着它前面的句子（里面包含了前三个■的位置）应该讲的是older form of manufacturing，而本题要求■的前句话是new form of manufacturing, 所以前三个■的位置均错。只能选第四个■的位置。

本题解题思路2：

第四个■的前句话：After 1815 this older form of manufacturing began to give way to factories...，而factories是对This new form of manufacturing的同义表达。因此，第四个■位置正确。

12

此类题型只考查细节定位能力：

Before 1815	1815–1850
(2) 第二段内容	(3) 最后一段内容
(6) 第二段内容	(5) 第三段内容
	(7) 第四段内容

(1) (4)均为错误选项，因为这两个选项均未被原文提及。

本文词汇总结

agitation	*n.*	骚动，不安
apprentice	*n.*	学徒
artisan	*n.*	技工，工匠
availability	*n.*	可获取性，可用性
bond	*n.*	联结，联系
burst	*n.*	突发
constant	*adj.*	稳定的，不变的
craftworker	*n.*	工匠
depression	*n.*	经济萧条
discard	*v.*	放弃，抛弃
disciplined	*adj.*	遵守纪律的
disrupt	*v.*	打扰，打乱
elegant	*adj.*	优美的，雅致的
fundamental	*adj.*	重要的，根本的
impart	*v.*	传授
journeyman	*n.*	学徒期满的职工
momentum	*n.*	势头，冲劲
necessitate	*v.*	使成为必须
obedience	*n.*	遵守，遵从
quit	*v.*	辞职；退出
regimented	*adj.*	受到严格控制的
resent	*v.*	憎恶，愤恨
steady	*adj.*	稳定的，平稳的
stimulate	*v.*	刺激；激发，促进
supervisory	*adj.*	监督的，管理的
symbol	*n.*	象征

Practice Set 6
SWIMMING MACHINES

文章结构

标 题	游泳“机器”
第一段	金枪鱼、鲭鱼和长嘴鱼一生都在游泳，它们身体的每一部分构造都让其成为当之无愧的游泳“机器”。
第二段	这些鱼的许多身体特性都是为减少水的阻力而形成的。
第三段	体形、眼睛、鳍的构造都利于减小水的阻力。
第四段	长长的鱼嘴利于它们在水中顺利穿行。
第五段	大多数金枪鱼和长嘴鱼胸部有鱼鳞，靠近尾巴处有龙骨脊和小鳍，这三个部位的作用也是减小水的阻力。
第六段	金枪鱼的腮的作用，以及它们不断游泳的原因。
第七段	金枪鱼的一个构造缺陷：一直张嘴呼吸降低了速度。
第八段	除了能够减小阻力之外，这些鱼还具有增加水的推动力的身体构造。鱼尾就是最高效的推动器。
第九段	这些鱼类具有保持体温的高效身体机制。

题目解析

1

<u>ENHANCE</u>

To **enhance** something means to improve its value, quality, or attractiveness.

同义词：improve, boost, increase, reinforce, strengthen

USE

If you **use** something, you do something with it in order to do a job or to achieve a particular result or effect.

同义词：apply, operate, practise, utilize, employ

IMPROVE

If something **improves** or if you improve it, it gets better.

同义词：enhance, advance, upgrade

COUNTERACT

To counteract something means to reduce its effect by doing something that produces an opposite effect.

同义词：act against, frustrate, offset, resist

BALANCE

① If you balance something somewhere, or if it balances there, it remains steady and does not fall.

② If you balance one thing with something different, each of the things has the same strength or importance.

同义词：stabilize, match, steady

通过上面五个单词的意义对比，可以得出与enhance意义最接近的是选项(B) improve。

另外，大家还需要记住：

【考】enhance = intensify

【英】to increase or improve (something)

【汉】*v.* 加强，提高

【预】boost, heighten, increase, strengthen

【例】The company is looking to **enhance** its potential earnings.

2

指代题

定位句：When not in use, the fins are tucked into special grooves or depressions so that they lie flush with the body and do not break up its smooth contours.

本题可以将(C)(D)两选项直接排除，它们在原文中是用“or”连接的。该解题思路的讲解详见练习五第十题。

选项(A)出现在定位句以外，且该选项代入原文后完全无法理解，因而也可以将其排除。

故本题正确答案为选项(B) fins。

3

关键词： airplanes retract their landing gear while in flight

定位句： Airplanes retract their landing gear while in flight for the **same** reason.

解题思路： 直选法

(D) To demonstrate a **similarity** in design between certain fishes and airplanes.

本题原文中强调的内容为“same reason”，而选项(D)强调的内容为“similarity”，两者的意义相互对应。该解题思路具体可见练习一第一题选项(C)的讲解。

错误选项讲解：

(A) To show that air resistance and water resistance work ~~differently~~ from each other.

原文强调“same”，一看到该选项中的“differently”就可将其直接排除掉，因为它与原文强调的重点不同。

(B) To argue that some fishes are ~~better~~ designed ~~than~~ airplanes are.

原文中是同级比较（same），而答案中却是异级比较（better than），与原文不对应，故可直接排除。

(C) To provide evidence that airplane ~~engineers have studied the design of fish bodies~~.

划删除线部分未被本段提及，故将其排除。

4

SOPHISTICATED

① A **sophisticated** machine, device, or method is more advanced or complex than others.

② Someone who is **sophisticated** is comfortable in social situations and knows about culture, fashion, and other matters that are considered socially important.

③ A **sophisticated** person is intelligent and knows a lot, so that they are able to understand complicated situations.

同义词：complex, complicated, intricate, refined, cultured

COMPLEX

详见练习二第三题解析。

AMAZING

You say that something is **amazing** when it is very surprising and makes you feel pleasure, approval, or wonder.

同义词：astonishing, surprising, stunning, overwhelming

CREATIVE

A **creative** person has the ability to invent and develop original ideas, especially in the arts.

同义词：imaginative, gifted, ingenious, inventive, original

PRACTICAL

The **practical** aspects of something involve real situations and events, rather than just ideas and theories.

同义词：functional, applied, empirical, pragmatic, realistic

通过上面五个单词的意义对比，可以得出与sophisticated意义最接近的是选项(A) complex。

另外，大家还需要记住：

【考】sophisticated = elaborate

【考】sophisticated = refined

【英】highly developed and complex

【汉】*adj.* 复杂的；精致的

【预】advanced, complicated, delicate, intricate

【例】Her knitting technique is more **sophisticated** than mine.

5

关键词：the long bills of marlins, sailfish, and swordfish probably help these fishes

定位句：The long bill of marlins, sailfishes, and swordfish probably helps them slip through the water.

解题思路：排除法

(A) increasing their ability to ~~defend themselves~~

(B) allowing them to ~~change direction~~ easily

(C) increasing their ability to ~~detect odors~~

划删除线部分均为定位句未提及的内容，可全被排除。

故选项(D)为正确答案。

6

关键词：tunas, in constant motion

定位句：They must also keep swimming to keep from sinking, since most have largely or completely lost the swim bladder, the gas-filled sac that helps most other fish remain buoyant.

解题思路：直选法

(A) They lack a swim bladder.

此选项内容与原文定位句内容完全一致，必为正确答案。

7

本题的考点在于考查**平行并列关系**。具体讲解见练习二第十题。

One potential problem is that opening the mouth to breathe detracts from the streamlining of these fishes and tends to slow them down.

其中“detracts”和“tends”是平行并列的关系。

这句话可以翻译为：一个潜在的问题是张开嘴呼吸会破坏这些鱼的流线形体，并且使它们的游行速度减慢。

选项(D)可以翻译为：张开嘴呼吸会使这些鱼的游行速度减慢。与原文意义相同，故正确。

选项(A)的错误在于，原文意思为整个这件事是一个problem，并不是opening the mouths有problem。

(B)(C)两选项的错误原因都是没有弄清楚原文中的平行并列关系。在原因中streamlining和slow down处于平行并列的关系中，它们之间没有任何动作关系。

8

CHANNEL

① If you **channel** money or resources into something, you arrange for them to be used for that thing, rather than for a wider range of things.

② If you **channel** our energies or emotions into something, you concentrate on or do that one thing, rather than a range of things.

同义词：direct, conduct, convey, guide, transmit

REDUCE

If you **reduce** something, you make it smaller in size or amount, or less in degree.

同义词：decrease, diminish, lower

REMOVE

If you **remove** something from a place, you take it away.

同义词：eliminate, displace, erase

DIRECT

① If you **direct** someone somewhere, you tell them how to get there.

② When someone **directs** a project or a group of people, they are responsible for organizing the people and activities that are involved.

同义词：guide, indicate, lead, control, manage

PROVIDE

If you **provide** something that someone needs or wants, or if you **provide** them **with** it, you give it to them or make it available to them.

同义词：supply, furnish

通过上面五个单词的意义对比，可以得出与channel意义最接近的是选项(C) direct。

9

关键词：one of the adaptations of fast-swimming fishes, these fishes' ability to

定位句：Perhaps most important of all to these and other fast swimmers is their ability to sense and make use of swirls and eddies (circular currents) in the water.

解题思路：直选法

(B) make efficient use of water currents

与原文定位句内容完全一致，为正确答案。

10

关键词：bluefin tunas

定位句：A blue-fin tuna in water of 7° C (45° F) can maintain a core temperature of over 25° C (77° F).

解题思路：直选法

(C) They can swim in waters that are much colder than their own bodies.

本题为数字考点的第二种情况（数字考点的具体讲解见练习三第十题），直接将“7° C (45° F) ”与“over 25° C (77° F)”作比较，可得出tunas can swim in waters that are colder than their bodies，即选项(C)。

错误选项讲解：

选项(D)虽然被原文提及：They have evolved special “heaters” of modified muscle tissue that warm the eyes and brain, maintaining peak performance of these critical organs. 但这句

话里的they是指它前句中的billfishes，并不是本题中的bluefin tunas，故错误。关于这个“选项陷阱”的讲解详见练习一第七题。

11

Consequently, ...

这个结构要求■的前句话是tunas do not need to suck in water的原因。

第二个■的前句话指明：只要tunas张开嘴，水就会被压进他们的腮里。这也就是“tunas不需要吸水”的原因。所以第二个■为正确答案。

第三个■不可以成为正确答案。在原文没有该句的情况下其关系为：只要tunas张开嘴，水就会被压进他们的腮里。相应地，它们也就丧失了大部分其他鱼用来吸水的肌肉。即：不需要吸水是丧失肌肉的原因。若把该句放在第三个■的位置，所表达的逻辑关系为：tunas丧失了大部分其他鱼用来吸水的肌肉，因此，他们就不需要吸水了。颠倒了原文要表明的因果关系。

12

此类题型考查细节定位能力。

REDUCING WATER RESISTANCE	INCREASING THRUST
(1) 原文第三段第三行信息：Most species lack scales over most of the body, making it smooth and slippery. (4) 原文第三段第四行信息：The eyes lie flush with the body and do not protrude at all. (5) 原文第三段第五行信息：The fins are stiff, smooth, and narrow, qualities that also help cut drag.	(2) 原文第八段第四行信息：Perhaps most important of all to these and other fast swimmers is their ability to sense and make use of swirls and eddies in the water. (7) 原文第八段第二行信息：Their high, narrow tails with swept-back tips are almost perfectly adapted to provide propulsion with the least possible effort.

(3) (6)两个选项均未被原文提及，故为错误选项。

本文词汇总结

buoyant	*adj.*	有浮力的，能漂浮的
compact	*adj.*	（体格）结实的
contour	*n.*	外形，轮廓
courtship	*n.*	求偶；求爱
depression	*n.*	凹陷（处）
detract	*v.*	降低，减损
drag	*n.*	阻力
eddy	*n.*	旋涡，涡流
enhance	*v.*	加强
protrude	*v.*	凸出，伸出
resemble	*v.*	与…相似，像
resistance	*n.*	阻力
retract	*v.*	缩进，收回
sleek	*adj.*	光滑的
slippery	*adj.*	滑溜的，光滑的
stiff	*adj.*	坚硬的，不易弯曲的
sophisticated	*adj.*	复杂的
supersonic	*adj.*	超音速的
swirl	*n.*	旋涡，涡流
thrust	*n.*	推力

Authentic TOEFL Practice Test 1

Passage 1

NINETEENTH-CENTURY POLITICS IN THE UNITED STATES

文章结构

标 题	19世纪的美国政治
第一段	美国现代总统制度始于安德鲁·杰克逊执政时期，他重新定义了美国总统的权力以及总统与民众的关系。
第二段	在安德鲁·杰克逊的第二任期中，他的反对者联合起来组建了辉格党，与他所代表的民主党在对待市场经济的态度上存在很大的分歧。
第三段	与民主党不同，辉格党认为市场经济会给全民带来好处。
第四段	辉格党和民主党的不同立场不仅体现在对市场作用的认识上，也体现在对中央政府职能的认识上。
第五段	与民主党不同，辉格党对政府所起的作用持积极的态度。
第六段	在社会基础的构成方面，辉格党和民主党存在相似之处。

题目解析

1

IMMEASURABLY

You use **immeasurably** to emphasize the degree or extent of a process or quality.

同义词：enormously, considerably, immensely, remarkably, tremendously, vastly

FREQUENT（→ FREQUENTLY）

If something is **frequent**, it happens often.

同义词：common, recurrent, repeated, customary

GREATLY

You use **greatly** to emphasize the degree or extent of something.

同义词：enormously, considerably, immensely, remarkably, tremendously, vastly

RAPID（→ RAPIDLY）

① A **rapid** change is one that happens very quickly.

② A **rapid** movement is one that is very fast.

同义词：quick, swift, brisk

REPORTEDLY

If you say that something is **reportedly** true, you mean that someone has said that it is true, but you have no direct evidence of it.

通过上面五个单词的意义对比，可以得出与immeasurably意义最接近的是选项(B) greatly。

2

关键词：the presidency of Andrew Jackson

定位句：The development of the modern presidency in the United States began with Andrew Jackson, who swept to power in 1829 at the head of the Democratic Party and served until 1837.

解题思路：直选法

(C) It was the beginning of the modern presidency in the United States.

本选项为原文定位句的同义转述，必为正确答案。

3

关键词：bankers and investors

定位句：This “paper money aristocracy” of bankers and investors manipulated the banking system for their own profit, Democrats claimed, and sapped the nation's virtue by encouraging speculation and the desire for sudden, unearned wealth.

解题思路：直选法

(B) The people that Democrats claimed were unfairly becoming rich

错误选项排除：

(A) The Democratic Party's main ~~source of support~~

(C) The people ~~most interested~~ in ~~a return to a simple agrarian republic~~

(D) One of the ~~groups in favor of~~ Andrew Jackson's presidency

4

关键词：commerce and economic development

定位句：For them, commerce and economic development were agents of civilization... Economic growth would benefit everyone by raising national income and expanding opportunity.

解题思路：直选法

(A) They would promote the advancement of society as a whole.

这个选项是原文定位句的同义表达(civilization, raising national income and expanding opportunity = advancement of society)，必为正确答案。

错误选项排除：

(B) They would ~~cause disagreements between Whigs and Democrats~~.

(C) They would ~~supply new positions~~ for Whig Party members.

(D) They would ~~prevent~~ conflict between farmers and workers.

5

关键词：Whig Party's view of the role of government

定位句：The government's responsibility was to provide a well-regulated economy that guaranteed opportunity for citizens of ability.

解题思路：直选法

(C) To maintain an economy that allowed all capable citizens to benefit

此选项是原文定位句的同义表达，必为正确答案。

错误选项排除：

(A) To ~~regulate the continuing conflict~~ between farmers and businesspeople

(B) To ~~restrict the changes~~ brought about by the market

(D) To ~~reduce the emphasis~~ on economic development

以上三个选项划删除线部分都为原文定位句未提及的内容，故均错。

6

INCLINATION

An **inclination** is a feeling that makes you want to act in a particular way.

同义词：tendency, disposition, penchant

ARGUMENT

① An **argument** is a statement or set of statements that you use in order to try to convince people that your opinion about something is correct.

② An **argument** is a discussion or debate in which a number of people put forward different or opposing opinions.

同义词：controversy, disagreement, dispute, discussion, assertion, debate, claim

TENDENCY

A **tendency** is a worrying or unpleasant habit or action that keeps occurring.

同义词：inclination, disposition, leaning

EXAMPLE

An **example of** something is a particular situation, object, or person which shows that what is being claimed is true.

同义词：specimen, case, illustration, sample

WARNING

A **warning** is something which is said or written to tell people of a possible danger, problem, or other unpleasant thing that might happen.

同义词：caution, alarm, alert, notification

通过上面五个单词的意义对比，可以得出与inclination意义最接近的是选项(B) tendency.

另外，大家还需要记住：

【考】be inclined = tend

【英】to think or to cause (someone) to think that something is probably true or correct

【汉】*adj.* 倾向于…的，有…意向的

【预】apt, prone, willing

【例】I am **inclined** to agree with you.

7

关键词：Democrat, support government action

定位句：Despite Andrew Jackson's inclination to be a strong President, Democrats as a rule believed in limited government. Government's role in the economy was to promote competition by destroying monopolies and special privileges.

解题思路：直选法

(C) Destroying monopolies

此选项是定位句的同义表达。

8

CONCEPT

A **concept** is an idea or abstract principle.

同义词：idea, abstraction, conception, notion

POWER

If someone has **power**, they have a lot of control over people and activities.

同义词：control, authority, dominance

REALITY

You use **reality** to refer to real things or the real nature of things rather than imagined, invented, or theoretical ideas.

同义词：truth, actuality, fact, realism, validity

DIFFICULTY

A **difficulty** is a problem.

同义词：hardship, arduousness, problem

IDEA

① An **idea** is a plan, suggestion, or possible course of action.

② An **idea** is an opinion or belief about what something is like or should be like.

同义词：thought, concept, impression, notion

通过上面五个单词的意义对比，可以得出与concept意义最接近的是选项(D) idea。

9

关键词：variations in political beliefs within the Whig Party

定位句：The Whigs, in contrast, viewed government power positively. They believed that..., and that.... In particular, Whigs in the **northern sections** of the United States also believed that...

解题思路：排除法

(A) They were ~~focused~~ on issues of public liberty.

(B) They caused ~~some members to leave the Whig Party~~.

(C) They were ~~unimportant~~ to most Whigs.

以上三个选项中的删除线部分在原文中均未被提及，所以错误。

正确答案为选项：(D) They reflected regional interests.

与定位句中下划线部分内容相对应，northern sections of the United States强调地域性差别（regional interests）。

10

NOT/EXCEPT题型

本题用此题型的两种解题方法都可以，如下：

思路1：解题方法2

(B) planters involved in international trade

Whigs appealed to planters who needed credit to finance their cotton and rice trade in the world market, to farmers who were eager to sell their surpluses, and to workers who wished to improve themselves.

这句话中下划线的部分就是选项(B)的同义表达，指出了Whigs的支持对象，本题问哪个不是Democrats的支持对象，故可直接选(B)。

思路2：解题方法1

(B) planters involved in international trade

其余三个选项均在Democrats部分被原文提及。

Democrats attracted farmers isolated from the market or uncomfortable with it, workers alienated from the emerging industrial system [选项(A)出处] , and rising entrepreneurs [选项(C)出处] who wanted to break monopolies and open the economy to newcomers [选项(D)出处] like themselves.

11

本题只有选项(D)中的while与原文中whereas相对应，引导对比转折关系。两者的对应关系如下：

The Whigs were strongest in the towns, cities and those rural areas that were fully integrated into the market economy, **whereas** Democrats dominated areas of semisubsistence farming that were more isolated and languishing economically.

The Democrats' power was greatest in poorer areas, **while** the Whigs were strongest in those areas where the market was already fully operating.

12

本句中含有“this...”这个结构，此结构的解题思路见练习一第12题中的具体讲解。

This new party 这个概念必须在■的前句话被提及。第一个■的前句话：During Jackson's second term, his opponents had gradually come together to form the Whig party. 而the Whig party是对this new party的同义表达。因此，第一个■位置正确。

13

提示句：The political system of the United States in the mid-nineteenth century was strongly influenced by the social and economic circumstances of the time.

(1)	✔	全文主旨内容。
(2)	✘	错误信息，与原文不符。
(3)	✘	错误信息，与原文不符。
(4)	✘	与原文主旨无关。
(5)	✔	二、三段主旨内容。
(6)	✔	四、五段主旨内容。

本文词汇总结

aristocrat	*n.*	贵族
aristocracy	*n.*	上层社会；贵族政治
agrarian	*adj.*	农村的；农业的
conflict	*n.*	冲突
dominance	*n.*	统治；支配
guarantee	*v.*	保证，确保
humanitarian	*adj.*	博爱的；人道主义的
inclination	*n.*	倾向，趋势
manipulate	*v.*	操纵，控制
monopoly	*n.*	垄断
presidency	*n.*	总统职位，主席职位
privilege	*n.*	特权
promote	*v.*	推广，促进
representative	*n.*	代表
sacrifice	*v.*	牺牲
sap	*v.*	削弱，消耗
speculation	*n.*	投机（买卖）
sweep	*v.*	一举获胜
opponent	*n.*	反对者
oppose	*v.*	反对

Passage 2
THE EXPRESSION OF EMOTIONS

文章结构

标 题	情感的表达
第一段	许多情感的表达方式是普遍一致的。
第二段	大多数调查显示，一些面部表情所传递的情感信息对所有人来说是一致的。
第三段	心理学家认为，面部表情是情感的一种表达；另外，面部表情还可以反作用于情感变化。
第四段	心理学实验研究证实，面部表情对情感有影响。
第五段	面部表情和情感的可能性联系。
第六段	英国英语的一个表达反映了面部表情对情感的作用。

题目解析

1

DESPONDENT

If you are **despondent**, you are very UNHAPPY because you have been experiencing difficulties that you think you will not be able to overcome.

同义词：depressed, sad

CURIOUS

If you describe something as **curious**, you mean that is unusual or difficult to understand.

同义词：unusual, bizarre, mysterious, peculiar, strange

THOUGHTFUL

If you are **thoughtful**, you are quiet and serious because you are thinking about something.

同义词：pensive

UNCERTAIN

If something is **uncertain**, it is not known or definite.

同义词：unsure, unclear, unconfirmed, undecided

通过上面五个单词的意义对比，可以得出与despondent意义最接近的是选项(B) unhappy。

2

关键词：Baring the teeth in a hostile way

定位句：It turns out that the expression of many emotions may be universal. Smiling is apparently a universal sign of friendliness and approval. Baring the teeth in a hostile way, as noted by Charles Darwin in the nineteenth century, may be a universal sign of anger.

解题思路：直选法

(C) provide an example of a facial expression whose meaning is widely understood

在原文定位句中，“baring the teeth in a hostile way...”与其前句“smiling is...”所起的作用是相同的，都是作为例子说明第一句话“it turns out that the expression of many emotions may be universal”。可见，只有选项(C)指明了这种关系，为正确答案。

3

CONCUR

If one person **concurs with** another person, the two people **AGREE**. You can also say that two people concur.

同义词：agree, assent, consent

ESTIMATE

If you **estimate** a quantity or value, you make an approximate judgment or calculation of it.

同义词：evaluate, guess

EXPECT

If you **expect** something to happen, you believe that it will happen.

同义词：look forward to, anticipate

UNDERSTAND

If you **understand** someone or **understand** what they are saying, you know what they mean.

同义词：comprehend, conceive

通过上面五个单词的意义对比，可以得出与concur意义最接近的是选项(B) agree。

4

定位句： In classic research Paul Ekman took photographs of people exhibiting the emotions of anger, disgust, fear, happiness, and sadness. He then asked people around the world to indicate what emotions were being depicted in them.

译文： 在典型的研究中，Ekman拍了一些带有生气、厌恶、恐惧、高兴和悲哀表情的人们的照片。然后，他让来自世界各地的人说出这些照片中人们分别表达了什么样的情感。

很明显，"them"的指代对象为选项(C) photographs。

5

关键词： Fore people of New Guinea

定位句： Those queried ranged from European college students to members of the Fore, a tribe that dwells in the New Guinea highlands. All groups, including the Fore, who had almost no contact with Western culture, agreed on the portrayed emotions.

解题思路： 直选法

(C) They knew very little about Western culture.

had almost no contact with Western culture = knew very little about Western culture

6

句子主干：The Fore also displayed familiar facial expressions when...if...

解题思路：排除法

(A) The Fore's facial expressions ~~indicated~~ their ~~unwillingness~~ to pretend to be story characters.

(B) The Fore ~~were asked to display~~ familiar facial expressions when they told their stories.

(D) The Fore ~~were familiar with~~ the facial expressions and basic emotions of characters in stories.

以上三选项均与原文主干不符，即不可能是原文的同义转述，必错。故选项(C)为正确答案，与原文主干内容相同。

7

关键词：Darwin, human emotions that were not expressed

定位句：Consider Darwin's words: "The free expression by outward signs of an emotion intensifies it. On the other hand, the repression, as far as possible, of all outward signs softens our emotions."

解题思路：直选法

(A) They would become less intense.

本选项是原文的同义转述（become less intense = soften）。另外，通过on the other hand可以判断出，后面的句子与前句表述的内容相反，即动词softens与intensifies表达的内容应该相反，从而可以推断出soften = less intense。

8

关键词：facial-feedback hypothesis

定位句：Psychological research has given rise to some interesting findings concerning the facial-feedback hypothesis. Causing participants in experiments to smile, for example, leads them to report more positive feelings and to rate cartoons as being more humorous.

解题思路：直选法

(A) The reactions of people in experiments to cartoons

此选项就是原文定位句下划线部分的概括性表达，必为正确答案。

9

RATE

If you **rate** someone or something as good or bad, you consider them to be good or bad. You can also say that someone or something **rates** as good or bad.

同义词：evaluate, consider, judge, measure

JUDGE

If you **judge** something, you guess its amount, size, or value or you guess what it is.

同义词：consider, assess, estimate, evaluate, rate, value

REJECT

If you **reject** something such as a proposal, a request, or an offer, you do not accept it or you do not agree to it.

同义词：deny, decline, veto, exclude, renounce

通过上面三个单词的意义对比，可以得出与rate意义最接近的是选项(A) judge。

另外，大家还需要记住：

【考】rate = evaluate

【英】to make a judgment about the quality, ability, or value of

【汉】*v.* 评估，评价；给…定级

【预】consider, count, estimate, measure, rank

【例】Judges **rated** each song according to a number of criteria.

10

RELEVANT

Something that is **relevant** to a situation or person is important or significant in that situation or to that person.

同义词：related, significant

CONTRADICTORY

If two or more facts, ideas, or statements are **contradictory**, they state or imply that opposite things are true.

同义词：inconsistent, contrary, opposed, opposite, conflicting

CONFUSING

Something that is **confusing** makes it difficult for people to know exactly what is happening or what to do.

同义词：bewildering, misleading, perplexing, puzzling, unclear

DEPENDENT

If one thing is **dependent** on another, the first thing will be affected or determined by the second.

同义词：relying on, reliant, subject to

APPLICABLE

Something that is **applicable** to a particular situation is relevant to it or can be applied to it.

同义词：relevant, suitable, useful

通过上面五个单词的意义对比，可以得出与relevant意义最接近的是选项(D) applicable。

11

关键词：stiffening the upper lip

定位句：Ekman's observation may be relevant to the British expression "keep a stiff upper lip" as a recommendation for handling stress. **It might be** that a "stiff" lip suppresses emotional response—as long as the lip is not quivering with fear or tension. But when the emotion that leads to stiffening the lip is more intense, and involves strong muscle tension, facial feedback **may heighten** emotional response.

解题思路：直选法

(D) It may either heighten or reduce emotional response.

这种"either... or..."句型与原文中"It might...But...may..."所表达的逻辑关系一致。

12

本句中含有"this..."这个结构，此结构的解题思路见练习一第12题中的具体讲解。

This universality in the recognition of emotions 这个概念必须在■的前句话被提及。

第三个■的前句话：Moreover, people in diverse cultures recognize the emotions manifested by the facial expressions. 这句话是对This universality in the recognition of emotions 所表达意思的重述。因此，第三个■位置正确。

13

提示句：Psychological research seems to confirm that people associate particular facial expressions with the same emotions across cultures.

(1)	✘	第六段细节信息用来支持"links between facial expressions and emotion may involve changes in brain temperature and the release of neurotransmitters"这个观点。
(2)	✔	第三、四段核心内容。
(3)	✘	原文未提及内容，错误。
(4)	✔	第三段首句，且为该段的核心内容。

(5)	✘	原文未提及内容，错误。
(6)	✔	第三、四段核心内容

本文词汇总结

arousal	*n.*	激发；激励；唤醒
bare	*v.*	露出
concur	*v.*	同意
despondent	*adj.*	沮丧的，垂头丧气的
depict	*v.*	描述
feedback	*n.*	反馈
frowning	*n.*	皱眉
hostile	*adj.*	敌对的，怀敌意的
intense	*adj.*	强烈的，剧烈的
intensify	*v.*	使强烈，加强
manifest	*v.*	显示，表示
multiple	*adj.*	多样的，多重的
originator	*n.*	创作者，发明人
participant	*n.*	参与者，参加者
perception	*n.*	感觉，知觉
preparedness	*n.*	作好准备
query	*v.*	询问，提问
reflect	*v.*	反映，表达
subtle	*adj.*	细微的；微妙的
universal	*adj.*	普遍的

Passage 3
GEOLOGY AND LANDSCAPE

文章结构

标 题	地质学与地形
第一段	地球是一个动态的球体，引起地形变化的原因主要有两个：建设性作用和破坏性作用。
第二段	现在越高的山峰，形成的时间越晚；而较低的山峰形成的时间较早，是一些高山的残骸。
第三段	山峰形成的三种模式：地球板块碰撞、地震和火山活动。
第四段	地形是建设性作用和破坏性作用相互影响的一种短暂体现。
第五段	气候是破坏性作用的主要媒介，如雨、二氧化碳。
第六段	其他气候因素以及生命体对地形的影响。

题目解析

1

关键词：changes in Earth's landscape

定位句：Most people consider the landscape to be unchanging, but Earth is a dynamic body, and its surface is continually altering—slowly on the human time scale, but relatively rapidly when compared to the great age of Earth (about 4.5 billion years).

解题思路：直选法

(D) They occur quickly in geological terms.

本选项为原文定位句的同义转述。

错误选项讲解：

(A) They occur ~~more often by uplift than by erosion~~.

(B) They occur only ~~at special times~~.

(C) They occur ~~less frequently~~ now than they once did.

上述三个选项划删除线的内容都是原文定位句未曾提及的内容，故可以直接排除。

另外，原文定位句中并不存在比较，但在(A)(C)两选项中都出现了比较级，符合错误选项的判断原则，故亦可排除。

2

RELATIVELY

Relatively means to a certain degree, especially when compared with other things of the same kind.

同义词：comparatively, rather, somewhat

UNUSUALLY

① You use **unusually** to emphasize that someone or something has more of a particular quality than is usual.

② You can use **unusually** to suggest that something is not what normally happens.

同义词：extraordinarily, remarkably, exceptionally, unconventionally, differently, strangely

COMPARATIVE (→ **COMPARATIVELY**)

You use **comparative** to show that you are judging something against a previous or different situation. For example, **comparative** calm is a situation which is calmer than before or calmer than the situation in other places.

同义词：relative, by comparison, qualified

OCCASIONALLY

Occasionally means happening sometimes, but not regularly or often.

同义词：sometimes, at times, irregularly, once in a while

NATURALLY

You use naturally to indicate that you think something is very obvious and not at all surprising in the circumstances.

同义词：of course, certainly

通过上面五个单词的意义对比，可以得出与relatively意义最接近的是选项(B) comparatively。

3

本题有明确的逻辑关系词，故采取以下步骤解题。

解题第一步：主从句的逻辑关系要与原文一致。

原文：..., but... (让步转折关系), 只有选项(B) Although..., ...和选项(C) ..., but...符合让步转折关系，所以将选项(A)(D)排除。

解题第二步：句子主干与原文一致。

原文主干为：they tend to be relatively short-lived in geological terms.

选项(B)的主干为：hills and mountains exist for a relatively short period of geological time，与原文相符，故保留。

选项(C)的主干为：only for a short time，与原文一致，故保留。

解题第三步：辅助内容尽量与原文一致。

原文中的辅助内容为：hills and mountains are often regarded as the epitome of permanence, ...

选项(B)的辅助内容为：they seem permanent，与原文一致，故为正确答案。

选项(C)的辅助内容为：hills and mountains successfully resist the destructive forces of nature，与原文不符，故错误。

4

关键词：the mountains of the Himalayas

定位句：As a general rule, the higher a mountain is, the more recently it was formed; for example, the high mountains of the Himalayas are only about 50 million years old. Lower mountains tend to be older, and are often the eroded relics of much higher mountain chains. About 400 million years ago, when the present-day continents of North America and Europe were joined, the Caledonian mountain chain was the same size as the modern Himalayas.

解题思路：直选法

(B) At present, they are much higher than the mountains of the Caledonian range.

原文表明，在四亿年前Caledonian mountain和现在的Himalayas是一样高的，并且指明山越古老就越低，则现在的Caledonian mountain一定比它四亿年前的高度低。可见，现在的Caledonian mountain要比Himalayas低。

错误选项讲解：

(A) Their current height is not an indication of their age.

原文指明“山越高，就越年轻。（The higher a mountain is, the more recently it was formed.）”即山的高度是其年龄的体现。该选项与原文表述内容相反，因此错误。

(C) They were a uniform height about 400 million years ago.

原文只表明在四亿年前, Caledonian mountain 和**modern** Himalayas 一样高，至于在四亿年前 Himalayas多高，我们并不知道。所以该选项错误。

(D) They are not as high as the Caledonian mountains were 400 million years ago.

原文表明，现在的Himalayas和四亿年前的Caledonian mountains是一样高的。该选项与原文表述内容相反，必错。

5

RELIC

① If you refer to something or someone as a **relic** of an earlier period, you mean that they belong to that period but have survived into the present.

② A **relic** is something which was made or used a long time ago and which is kept for its historical significance.

同义词：remnant, remain, fragment

RESEMBLANCE

If there is a **resemblance** between two people or things, they are similar to each other.

同义词：similarity, likeness

REGION

A **region** is a large area of land that is different from other areas of land, for example because it is one of the different parts of a country with its own customs and characteristics, or because it has a particular geographical feature.

同义词：area, district, locality, territory

REMAIN

Historical **remains** are things that have been found from an earlier period of history, usually buried in the ground, for example parts of buildings and pieces of pottery.

同义词：relic, remnant, residue, debris, leftover

RESTORATION

When someone **restores** something such as an old building, painting, or piece of furniture, they repair and clean it, so that it looks like it did when it was new.

同义词：repair, reconstruction, renewal, renovation, revival

通过上面五个单词的意义对比，可以得出与relics意义最接近的是选项(C) remains。

另外，大家还需要记住：

【考】relic = remnant

【英】something that is from a past time, place, culture, etc.

【汉】*n.* 遗迹，残留物，残片

【预】fragment, trace

【例】There is a museum of war **relics**.

6

关键词：cause of mountain formation

定位句：Some mountains were formed as a result of these plates crashing into each other and forcing up the rock at the plate margins.

解题思路：直选法

(C) force of Earth's crustal plates hitting each other

本选项为原文定位句的同义转述。

错误选项讲解：

(A) effect of ~~climatic change~~ on sea level

(B) ~~slowing down~~ of volcanic activity

(D) ~~replacement of sedimentary rock~~ with volcanic rock

上述三个选项划删除线的内容都是原文定位句未曾提及的信息，均可直接排除。选项(B)强调火山活动速度slowing down (减缓)，但原文只提到火山活动，故错误。

7

关键词：Carbon dioxide

定位句：Carbon dioxide in the air reacts with the rainwater, forming a weak acid (carbonic acid) that may chemically attack the rocks.

解题思路：直选法

(A) To explain the origin of a chemical that can erode rocks

此选项与原文陈述内容一致。

此题易误选(C) To give an example of how rainwater penetrates soil，若(C)为正确选项，则该选项内容必须与carbon dioxide这句话的前句话内容一致。但其前句话为：Rain washes away loose soil and penetrates cracks in the rocks.（雨水冲走了疏松的土壤，渗透到岩石的缝隙中。）而(C)选项的内容却是：雨水如何渗透到土壤里。原文中雨水和土壤的关系是"wash away"而不是"penetrates"，内容不一致，且符合"混淆选项"的特征，故错误。详见练习三第七题"混淆选项特征"的讲解。

8

SEEP

If something such as liquid or gas **seeps** somewhere, it **FLOWS SLOWLY** and in small amounts into a place where it should not go.

同义词：permeate, soak, trickle

另外，大家还需要记住：

【考】seep = pass through slowly

【英】to flow or pass slowly through small openings in something

【汉】*v.* 渗漏

【预】ooze, exude, leak, permeate, soak

【例】The chemicals **seeped** into the ground.

9

方法1：

Glacier may form in permanently cold areas, and these slowly moving masses of ice cut out valleys, carrying **with them** huge quantities of eroded rock debris.

本句话等价于：

Glacier may form in permanently cold areas, and these slowly moving masses of ice cut out valleys, carrying huge quantities of eroded rock debris **with them**.

此时them必须指代carrying这个动作的发出者，即these slowly moving masses of ice，故本题选(B)。

方法2：

将四个选项分别代入原文进行翻译，(A)(C)(D)三个选项均无法使译文通顺，只有选项(B)可以，故(A)(C)(D)均错，本题仍应选(B)。

10

关键词：无

在没有关键词可定位的情况下，按“顺序原则”寻找原文定位句。

> **顺序原则**
> 在托福阅读中，题目的顺序一般是按照文章的顺序设置。即下一题的考点应该出在其前一题的定位句之后。

在本题中由于第九题考查内容为第六段的前半部分内容。因此本题可在第九题定位句之后寻找答案出处。

定位句：In dry areas the wind is the principal agent of erosion. It carries fine particles of sand, which bombard exposed rock surfaces, thereby wearing them into yet more sand.

译文：在干旱地区，风是破坏性作用的主要媒介。它带着细小的沙粒，这些沙粒不断地撞击岩石裸露的表面，从而又把岩石的表面磨成了更多的沙粒。

解题思路：直选法

(D) sand

11

在插入句中的“another type of destructive force”要求■前句话中必须在讲destructive force。而第一个■前面讲ice和frost是destructive force，符合要求。并且，两个“under...”的短语也构成了一种并列结构。故第一个■位置为正确答案。

12

此类题型考查细节定位能力。

CONSTRUCTIVE PROCESSES	DESTRUCTIVE PROCESSES
(1)原文第三段第二行信息：Some mountains were formed as a result of these plates crashing into each other and forcing up the rock at the plate margins. (5)原文第三段第五行信息：Other mountains may be raised by earthquakes, which fracture the Earth's crust and can displace enough rock to produce block mountains. (6)原文第三段第七行信息：A third type of mountain may be formed as a result of volcanic activity which occurs in regions of active fold mountain belts, such as in the Cascade Range of western North America.	(3) 原文第六段第三行信息：In dry areas the wind is the principal agent of erosion. It carries fine particles of sand, which bombard exposed rock surfaces, thereby wearing them into yet more sand. (7) 原文第五段第一行信息：The weather, in its many forms, is the main agent of erosion.

本文词汇总结

alter *v.* 变化，改变
Appalachians *n.* 阿巴拉契亚山脉（位于北美洲）
bombard *v.* 猛烈撞击
crack *n.* 缝隙
debris *n.* 碎片，残骸
deposit *v.* 沉积，沉淀
dynamic *adj.* 动态的
epitome *n.* 象征
erosion *n.* 侵蚀
fine *adj.* 细小的
fracture *v.* 使断裂
fragment *n.* 碎片
landscape *n.* 地貌
lava *n.* 熔岩
mass *n.* 堆，块
penetrate *v.* 渗透
permanence *n.* 永久，永恒
plateau *n.* 高原，高地
principal *adj.* 主要的
react *v.* 起化学反应
relic *n.* 残留物，遗迹
resist *v.* 抵抗，抵制
scale *n.* 范围，规模
seep *v.* 渗入
segment n. 部分
shatter *v.* 粉碎
split *v.* 分离，分裂
temporary *adj.* 暂时的
terrain *n.* 地形，地势
wear *v.* 磨损，耗损

Authentic TOEFL Practice Test 2

Passage 1

FEEDING HABITS OF EAST AFRICAN HERBIVORES

文章结构

标 题	东非食草动物的摄食习性
第一段	东非塞伦盖蒂平原的五大类哺乳动物都是食草动物，每类动物的食物范围都与其他有所差别。
第二段	造成这种摄食差别的主要原因有两个，其中之一是消化系统的不同。
第三段	另一个原因是身体体积的大小不同。
第四段	这些动物因各自不同的摄食习性也养成了不同的迁徙习惯。

题目解析

1

(C) misleading

ILLUSORY

If you describe something as **illusory**, you mean that although it seems true or possible, it is in fact false or impossible.

同义词: false, unreal, deceptive, fallacious, mistaken

注意：因为阅读部分的考点在前面的题目讲解过程中已经几乎全部涵盖，Authentic TOEFL Practice Test 2 & 3中的题目基本上是对前面各种考点的不断重复，所以这两部分的题目讲解相对前面来说比较简洁直接。请考生在看这两套题时，主动思考，多联系前面讲过的内容，举一反三，真正地理解那些重点解题思路。

2

(B) thinly

SPARSE（→ SPARSELY）

Something that is **sparse** is small in number or amount and spreads out over an area.

同义词：meagerly, thinly, scantly, rarely

另外，大家还需要记住：

【考】sparse = rare

【考】sparse = not rich

【英】present only in small amounts; less than necessary or normal

【汉】*adj.* 稀少的，零星的

【预】scattered, scanty, scarce

【例】Reliable data is **sparse**.

3

NOT/ EXCEPT 题型

原文只在括号部分中提及：(they did not study buffalo)。这之后没有再对其进行任何解释。故本题正确答案为选项(D) why were buffalo excluded from the research study?

4

(D) connected

ASSOCIATE(→ ASSOCIATED)

If you **associate** someone or something **with** another thing, the two are connected in your mind.

同义词: connect, combine, join, link

5

关键词：horse, cow

定位句：According to their digestive systems, these herbivores can be divided into two categories: the nonruminants (such as the zebra, which has a digestive system like a horse) and the ruminants (such as the wildebeest, topi, and gazelle, which are like the cow).

解题思路：直选法

(C) illustrate differences between ruminants and nonruminants through the use of animals likely to be familiar to most readers

原文定位句中括号内的horse和cow分别在为介绍nonruminants和ruminants这两种动物举例子，故直接选(C)。

6

关键词：large quantities of plant stems, quantity of food

定位句：**The zebra** chooses areas where there is more low-quality food. It migrates first to unexploited areas and chomps the abundant low-quality stems before moving on.

解题思路：直选法

(C) the zebra

7

关键词：differences in feeding preferences of East African herbivores

定位句：How are we to understand their different feeding preferences? The answer lies in two associated differences among the species, in their digestive systems and body sizes...They are ruminants and have a special structure (the rumen) in their stomachs, which contains microorganisms that can break down the hard parts of plants.

解题思路：直选法

(B) the differences in stomach structure

8

NOT/ EXCEPT 题型：

本题用第二种解题方法

(A) They digest their food very quickly.

此观点与原文表明的观点(Food passes **only slowly** through the ruminant's gut because...)相反，故错误。

9

(A) as long as

PROVIDED THAT

If you say that something will happen **provided** or **provided that** something else happens, you mean that the first thing will happen only if the second thing also happens.

同义词: on condition that, as long as, given, providing

10

(D) demanding

FASTIDIOUS

If you say that someone is **fastidious**, you mean that they pay great attention to detail because they like everything to be very neat, accurate, and in good order.

同义词： meticulous

11

定位句：The later species all depend on the preparations of the earlier one, <u>for the actions of **the zebra** alter the vegetation to suit the stomachs of the wildebeest, topi, and gazelle</u>.

解题思路：直选法

(B) zebra

12

关键词：wildebeests

定位句：The later species all depend on the preparations of the earlier one, for the actions of the zebra alter the vegetation to suit the stomachs of the wildebeests, topi, and gazelle.

解题思路：直选法

(C) They tend to choose feeding areas in which the vegetation has been worn down.

13

在插入句中的"they, their"要求■前句话中必须有其指代对象。

第四个■位置正确。they和their指代前句中的mammals，并且第四个■之后的句子正是按照body size讲述迁徙的顺序，完全符合逻辑关系；此外，sequence和order也相互呼应。

14

提示句：East African herbivores, though they all live in the same environment, have a range of feeding preferences.

(1)	✘	原文未提及。
(2)	✔	第三段主旨内容。
(3)	✘	原文未提及。
(4)	✔	第二段主旨内容。
(5)	✔	第四段主旨内容。
(6)	✘	与原文观点相反。原文第四段已经指明East African herbivores的迁徙方式

本文词汇总结

associated	*adj.*	相关的，相联系的
abundant	*adj.*	丰富的
chew	*v.*	咀嚼
colleague	*n.*	同事
content	*n.*	内容
digestive	*adj.*	消化的
distribute	*v.*	分布，分散
exploit	*v.*	开发，开拓
fastidious	*adj.*	挑剔的，苛求的
fuel	*v.*	给…补充能量
gazelle	*v.*	小羚羊，瞪羚
herbivore	*n.*	食草动物
illusory	*adj.*	虚假的
intermediate	*adj.*	居中的，中间的
likewise	*adv.*	同样地，也
mammal	*n.*	哺乳动物
metabolic	*adj.*	新陈代谢的
migratory	*adj.*	迁徙的
nutritious	*adj.*	有营养的
proportion	*n.*	比例
ruminant	*n.*	反刍动物
sparsely	*adv.*	稀疏地
stem	*n.*	茎，干
wildebeest	*v.*	牛羚
zebra	*n.*	斑马

Passage 2

LOIE FULLER

文章结构

标 题	洛伊 • 富勒
第一段	洛伊 • 富勒是一位美国舞蹈家。
第二段	她设计了一种舞蹈，着重表现灯光转换和色彩与舞蹈服装的相互辉映。
第三段	她成名于巴黎，深受巴黎观众和众多诗人、画家的喜爱。
第四段	她注重开发各种舞台技术，创造出了复合而多彩的舞台效果。
第五段	除了舞蹈形式之外，她也渐渐开始关注音乐本身，并展现出越来越宏大的主题。此外，她还参与了电影的拍摄。
第六段	洛伊 • 富勒对后来的舞蹈家和舞蹈艺术的创新作出了很大的贡献。

题目解析

1

关键词：theatrical dance in the late nineteenth century

定位句：The United States dancer Loie Fuller(1862-1928) found theatrical dance in the late nineteenth century artistically unfulfilling.

解题思路：直选法

(C) It was more a form of entertainment than a form of serious art.

原文指出，19世纪的舞蹈的艺术性还不够，与纯粹的艺术形式相比，它只是一种娱乐消遣的方式。

2

NOT/ EXCEPT题型

采用解题方法1。由于(A) (B) (C) 选项在原文中均被明确提及，故(D) 为正确选项。

定位句：Fuller devised a type of dance that focused on the shifting play of lights and colors[选项(A)出处] on the voluminous skirts or draperies [选项(B)出处] she wore, which she kept in constant motion principally through movements of her arms, sometimes extended with wands concealed under her costumes[选项(C) 出处].

3

(A) highly regarded

PRESTIGIOUS

A **prestigious** institution, job, or activity is respected and admired by people.

同义词: respected, notable, prominent

4

Although..., she was not primarily interested in storytelling or expressing emotions through dance; the drama of her dancing emanated from her visual effects.

(A) Fuller was more interested in dance's visual impact than in its narrative or emotional possibilities.

5

(C) hired

ENGAGE

If you **engage** someone to do a particular job, you appoint them to do it.

同义词: employ, hire, appoint, enlist

另外，大家还需要记住：

【考】engage = involve

【英】to take part in

【汉】*v.* 从事，参加

【预】participate, join, take part

【例】She **engaged** him in conversation.

6

(D) integrate

SYNTHESIZE

If you **synthesize** different ideas, facts, or experiences, you combine them to form a single idea or impression.

同义词：integrate, fuse

7

关键词：Fuller's work well received in Paris

定位句：..., she achieved her greatest glory in Paris, ... Many of her dances represented elements or natural objects—Fire, the Lily, the Butterfly, and so on—and thus accorded well with the fashionable Art Nouveau style, ...Her dancing also attracted the attention of French poets and painters of the period, for it appealed to their liking for mystery...

解题思路：直选法

(D) Fuller's dances were in harmony with the artistic values already present in Paris.

该选项是对原文定位句的总结性叙述。

8

关键词：*Fire Dance*

定位句：One of Fuller's major inventions was **underlighting**, in which she stood on a pane of frosted glass **illuminated from underneath**. This was particularly effective in her *Fire Dance* (1895),...

解题思路： 直选法

(C) technique of lighting the dancer from beneath

9

关键词： *The Sea*

定位句： As her technological expertise grew more sophisticated, so did the other aspects of her dances...She began to address more ambitious themes in her dances such as *The Sea*, in which her dancers invisibly agitated a huge expanse of silk, played upon by colored lights. Always open to scientific and technological innovations,...

解题思路： 排除法

(A) To point out a dance of Fuller's in which ~~music did not play an important role~~

删除线部分未被作者提及，与原文无关。

(B) To explain why Fuller sometimes used music by progressive composers

本题考点与more ambitious themes相关，与progressive composers没有任何关联，故该选项错误。

(D) To illustrate ~~how Fuller's interest in science was reflected in her work~~

删除线部分与原文无关。

故本题正确答案应为选项(C)。

10

(B) created movement in

AGITATE(→ AGITATED)

If you **agitate** something, you shake it so that it moves about.

同义词：churn, shake, discompose

另外，大家还需要记住：

【考】agitate = disturb

【英】to excite and often trouble the mind or feelings of

【汉】*v.* 扰乱，使不安

【预】stir, rouse

【例】Some members of the union have been **agitating** for a strike.

11

关键词：Fuller's theater, Paris Exposition

定位句：At the Paris Exposition in 1900, she had her own theater, where, in addition to her own dances, she presented pantomimes by the Japanese actress Sada Yocco.

解题思路：直选法

(A) It presented some works that were not by Fuller.

12

定位句：This was particularly effective in her ***Fire Dance***, performed to the music of Richard Wagner's "Ride of the Valkyries."

解题思路：直选法

(A) *Fire Dance*

13

题干中强调除dance以外的newly emerging artistic media。第四个■前面内容讲的是与dance相关的内容，而其后文讲的是film，符合该题目的逻辑关系，为正确选项。

14

提示句：Loie Fuller was an important and innovative dancer.

(1)	✘	原文未提及。
(2)	✘	原文未提及。
(3)	✔	
(4)	✔	
(5)	✔	
(6)	✘	原文未提及。

排除法思路： 由于本题(1)(2)(6)选项均未被原文提及，直接可被断定为错误选项，故剩余的其他三个选项必为正确答案。

本文词汇总结

address	*v.*	从事，表演
agitate	*v.*	摇动
ambitious	*adj.*	有雄心的，宏大的
appearance	*n.*	露面，出现
ballet	*n.*	芭蕾舞
befriend	*v.*	与…交朋友
canvas	*n.*	帆布，画布
constant	*adj.*	不变的，持续的
duet	*n.*	二重奏
element	*n.*	元素
engage	*v.*	使从事，使参与
establish	*v.*	建立
eventually	*adv.*	最后，终于
expertise	*n.*	专业知识
exposition	*n.*	博览会
extremely	*adv.*	非常，极其
fashionable	*adj.*	流行的，时髦的
glory	*n.*	荣耀
pane	*n.*	块，板
prestigious	*adj.*	有名望的
radium	*n.*	镭
shift	*v.*	转移，交替
sinuous	*adj.*	弯曲的
sophisticated	*adj.*	复杂的，精致的
theatrical	*adj.*	戏剧的
tribute	*n.*	致敬，献礼
virtuosity	*n.*	精湛技艺
voluminous	*adj.*	宽大的

Passage 3
GREEN ICEBERGS

文章结构

标　题	绿色的冰山
第一段	冰山是什么。
第二段	冰山的颜色。
第三段	冰山呈现出绿色的两种解释。
第四段	冰山呈现出绿色的第三种新解释。
第五段	绿色的冰山层由含有绿色生物物质的海水冰冻形成。
第六段	绿色的冰山与冰架分离，就会倒翻露出冰面。
第七段	埃默里冰架非常适合产生绿色冰山。

题目解析

1

NOT/ EXCEPT 题型

本题用第二种解题方法。

(C) Most of their mass is above the sea surface.

该选项很明显与原文观点相反，原文的表述为：they float with only about 12 percent of their mass above the sea surface. (它们仅仅有12%的部分漂浮在海面上。)

2

关键词：icebergs, dark, opaque

定位句：Icebergs are ordinarily blue to white, although they sometimes appear dark or opaque because they carry gravel and bits of rock.

解题思路：直选法

(B) the presence of gravel or bits of rock

3

本题含有明确的逻辑关系词，应按照前面介绍的“句子简化题”的三个步骤依次判断。

解题步骤一：主从句逻辑关系与原文尽量保持一致。

原文为“but”引导的让步转折关系，其中(A) (C) (D)三个选项与原文对应。

解题步骤二：主干与原文尽量保持一致。

原文中“but”后（Green icebergs stand out among white and blue icebergs under a great variety of light conditions）为主要强调内容。

选项(A)but后内容为：this is attributed to an optical illusion，与原文强调内容不符，故可排除。

选项(C)but后内容为：green icebergs stand out **best** among other icebergs **when illuminated by a near-horizon red Sun**，首先原文中不存在最高级best，而该选项自行添加，与原文不符，故错误。另外，该选项中when illuminated by a near-horizon red Sun为原文but前面的非强调内容，该选项将这部分内容放在but后，与原文不符，仍为错误标志。故可将选项(C)排除。

所以，本题正确选项为(D) One explanation attributes the color of green icebergs to an optical illusion under special light conditions, but green icebergs appear distinct from other icebergs under a great variety of light conditions.

4

(B) pierce

PENETRAT

If something or someone **penetrates** a physical object or an area, they succeed in getting into it or passing through it.

同义词: pierce, bore, go through, enter

另外，大家还需要记住：

【考】penetrate = enter

【英】to go through or into something

【汉】v. 穿入，穿透

【预】pierce, bore, go through

【例】The roots of these plants have been known to **penetrate** to a depth of more than 15 feet.

5

关键词：glacial ice, formed

定位句：The ice shelf cores, with a total length of 215 meters (705 feet), were long enough to penetrate through glacial ice—which is formed from the compaction of snow and contains air bubbles—and to continue into the clear, bubble-free ice formed from seawater that freezes onto the bottom of the glacial ice.

解题思路：直选法

(A) by the compaction of snow

6

定位句：The properties of this clear sea ice were very similar to the ice form the green iceberg.

解题思路：直选法

(D) the clear sea ice at the bottom of the ice shelf is similar to ice from a green iceberg

其中this clear sea ice指代前句中的the clear, bubble-free ice formed from seawater that freezes onto the bottom of the glacial ice。

7

本题不符合ETS习惯性的出题思路，不必仔细研究。

8

(A) collected

ACCUMULATE

When you **accumulate** things or when they **accumulate**, they collect or are gathered over a period of time.

同义词: collect, build up, gather, increase, store

另外，大家还需要记住：

【考】accumulate = pile up

【考】accumulate = build up

【英】to gather or pile up especially little by little

【汉】*v.* 积累，聚集

【预】amass, gather, increase

【例】Evidence of his guilt is **accumulating**.

9

(A) kept out

EXCLUDE

If you **exclude** someone **from** a place or activity, you prevent them from entering it or taking part in it.

同义词: keep out, ban, forbid, prohibit

10

(D) come together

11

NOT/ EXCEPT 题型

(B) Why blocks of shelf ice sometimes capsize after breaking off

原文只是指出：The scientists concluded that green icebergs form when a two-layer block of shelf ice breaks away and capsizes (turns upside down), exposing the bubble-free shelf ice that was formed from seawater. 在此之后，没有对这种现象进行任何进一步解释。故本题答案为选项(B)。

12

(C) The Amery Ice Shelf produces green icebergs because the seawater is rich in a particular kind of soluble organic material.

原文先在第六段指出：The slush is compacted by an unknown mechanism, and solid, bubble-free ice is formed from water high in soluble organic substance，这说明了green icebergs 呈现绿色的原因。紧接在第七段指出：The Amery Ice Shelf appears to be uniquely suited to the production of green icebergs，说明Amery Ice Shelf 这个地方有很多soluble organic substance，即选项(C)。

13

要插入原文的句子指出：科学家对冰山呈现绿色的原因有不同的解释：由于光线条件，还是冰内的物质。而整个第三段就是在阐述三个不同原因。故本题的正确答案为第二个■。

14

提示句：Several suggestions, ranging from light conditions to the presence of metallic compounds, have been offered to explain why some icebergs appear green.

(1)	✘	ice cores为第三个explanation的内容，metallic compounds including copper and iron为第二个explanation的内容，原文未将两者同时提及。故该选项为典型的混淆选项，必错。
(2)	✘	All ice shelves can produce green icebergs 这个观点未被原文提及，故错误。
(3)	✔	第四段主旨内容。
(4)	✔	第五段主旨内容。
(5)	✘	Green icebergs are white until...此概念未被原文提及，错误。
(6)	✔	第五段和第六段的主旨内容。

本文词汇总结

accrete	*v.*	增长
Antarctica	*n.*	南极洲
bubble	*n.*	气泡
current	*n.*	水流
detach	*v.*	分离
dissolved	*adj.*	溶解的
drift	*v.*	漂流，漂移
erosion	*n.*	侵蚀，腐蚀
explanation	*n.*	说明，解释
float	*v.*	浮动，飘浮
glacier	*n.*	冰川
gravel	*n.*	碎石，砂砾
illusion	*n.*	幻觉
inland	*n.*	内陆
irregular	*adj.*	不规则的
massive	*adj.*	大量的
melt	*v.*	融化
opaque	*adj.*	不透明的
partially	*adv.*	部分地
penetrate	*v.*	渗透
portion	*n.*	部分
related	*adj.*	有关系的
separate	*v.*	分开，隔开
shelf	*n.*	架子
soluble	*adj.*	可溶的
texture	*v.*	使…形成某种结构
variety	*n.*	多样

Authentic TOEFL Practice Test 3

Passage 1
ARCHITECTURE

文章结构

标 题	建 筑
第一段	建筑反映了人类的文化和价值观。
第二段	建筑是为人类的生活而服务的。
第三段	与建筑材料相比，建筑的结构长期以来变化较小。
第四段	建筑技术和建筑材料的变化影响着建筑行业的发展。
第五段	现代建筑的三大主要组成部分。
第六段	用石头作材料的建筑的特点和结构变化。

题目解析

1

NOT/EXCEPT题型

此题的正确答案为选项(D)。因为原文的最后一句话为 architecture **affects our lives most directly** for it determines the character of the human environment in major ways. 而选项(D)为：Architecture has an **indirect effect** on life，与原文的观点相反。

2

(B) improve

【考】enhance = **improve**

【考】enhance = intensify

【英】to increase or improve (something)

【汉】*v.* 加强，提高

【预】boost, heighten, increase, strengthen

【例】The company is looking to **enhance** its potential earnings.

3

(C) achievable

【考】feasible = practical

【考】feasible = possible

【英】possible to do

【汉】*adj.* 可实行的

【预】achievable, attainable, practicable, reasonable, viable

【例】This plan for a new town library is not economically **feasible**.

4

句子主干层次划分：

[In order for the structure to achieve the size and strength necessary to meet its purpose]❶, **architecture employs methods of support** [that, because they are based on physical laws❸, have changed little since people first discovered them—even while building materials have changed dramatically❹]❷.

句子主干：Architecture employs methods of support.

❶ 状语部分，为主句服务

❷ 定语从句修饰methods of support

❸ 原因状语从句修饰❷定语从句的主干that have changed little since people first discovered them

❹ 让步状语从句，其功能与❸相同。

译文：为使建筑结构达到满足需要所必需的大小和强度，建筑学运用了一些支撑的方法。

由于这些支撑的方法是建立在物理学定理基础之上的，所以尽管建筑材料已经发生了极大的变化，但这些支撑的方法自从人们发现它们那天起到目前为止就基本上没有发生任何变化。

选项(A)中的physical laws与the size and strength of building在原文中分别位于不同的意群，它们之间没有任何关系，而此选项将这两者建立了某种关系，必错。该选项为典型的错误选项类型之一：混淆选项。

选项(B)中的building materials have changed与architectural size and strength在原文中也是没有任何关联的，此选项将两者建立关联，必错。该选项亦为典型的混淆选项。

选项(C)主干the structural methods used to provide strength and size were inadequate原文未提及，必错。

故本题正确答案为选项(D)。

5

(B) created

【考】devise = **create**

【英】to form in mind by new ideas or principles

【汉】*v.* 设计，发明

【预】construct, design, formulate, invent

【例】They have **devised** a new method for converting sunlight into electricity.

6

(A) essential

【考】integral = **essential**

【英】very important and necessary

【汉】*adj.* 构成整体所必需的，基本的

【预】basic, component, constituent, fundamental, indispensable, necessary

【例】Industry is an **integral** part of modern society.

7

定位句： Materials and methods of construction are integral parts of the design of architecture structures. In earlier times it was necessary to design structural systems suitable for the materials that were available, such as wood, stone, or brick. **Today technology has progressed to the point where it is possible to invent new building materials to suit the type of structure desired**.

正确答案为选项(B)：建筑材料不再限制建筑结构的类型。原文定位句中指出材料和建筑方法都是设计建筑结构时需要考虑的重要因素。以前，建筑的设计要适合当时可以得到的材料；而如今，由于科技的进步，人们能够设计出新型的材料来满足建筑设计的需要，即材料能够得到与否不再限制建筑的设计。

错误选项分析：

选项(A)Because new building materials are ~~hard to find~~, construction techniques have changed very little from past generations. 划删除线内容在原文未提及，可以排除。

选项(C)与原文内容不一致。原文中的时间为in earlier times，但在选项中却为today，故错误。

选项(D)Architects in earlier times ~~did not have enough building materials~~ to enclose large spaces. 划删除线内容原文未提及，可以排除。

8

定位句： Enormous changes in materials and techniques of construction within the last few generations have made it possible to enclose space with much greater ease and speed and with a minimum of material. Progress in this area can be measured **by the difference in weight between buildings built now and those of comparable size that were built one hundred years ago**.

译文： 近几十年建筑材料和科学技术的巨大变化使得人们能用更简单、更快捷的方法和更少的材料来建造同等大小的建筑。这个方面的成就可以通过对比现在的建筑与100年前和它相同大小的建筑之间重量的差异体现出来。

文章指明，这种进步（即用更简单、更快捷的方法和更少的材料来建造同等大小的建筑）可以由对比现在的建筑与100年前和它相同大小的建筑之间重量的差异体现出来。也就是说，现在的建筑物要比100年前同样大小的建筑物在重量上更轻。故本题正确答案为选项(C)：在同等大小的情况下，现在的建筑要比100年前的建筑更轻。

错误选项分析：

(A) They occupy much ~~less space~~ than buildings constructed one hundred years ago.

(D) They take ~~a long time to build~~ as a result of their complex construction methods.

这两个选项的删除线部分未被原文提及，无法推断，故错误。

(B) They are not very different from the buildings of a few generations ago.

下划线部分与原文观点相反，故错误。

9

定位句： Modern architectural forms generally have three separate components comparable to elements of the human body: … .Of course in early architecture—such as igloos and adobe structures—there was no such equipment, and the skeleton and skin were often one.

文章先陈述现代建筑结构主要分为三个不同的部分，就像人体也是三个部分构成的一样；但在早期的建筑中，并不这样完整。由此可得出选项(D)为正确答案：总的来说，现代的建筑与早期建筑相比更类似于人体结构。

错误选项分析：

(A) ~~Complex equipment~~ inside buildings is the one element in modern architecture that resembles a component of the human body. 删除线内容未被原文提及，故排除。

(B) The components in early buildings were similar to three particular elements of the human body. 下划线部分与原文陈述不符，原文为modern buildings。

(C) Modern buildings have components that are as likely ~~to change as~~ the human body is. 删除线内容未被原文提及，故排除。

10

(A) difficult

【考】arduous = **difficult**

【英】hard to accomplish or achieve

【汉】*adj.* 艰巨的

【预】exhausting, fatiguing, tiring

【例】He went through a long and **arduous** training program.

11

定位句：The doorways and windows are made possible by placing over the open spaces thick stone beams that support the weight from above. A structural invention had to be made before the physical limitations of stone could be overcome and new architectural forms could be created. That invention was *arch*, a curved structure originally made of separate stone or brick segments.

译文：修建门和窗需要在开阔的空间上放置厚石板来支撑上面的石头。在创造出新的建筑形式之前，要克服石头的物理局限性，（建筑师们）必须发明出新的建筑结构。这就是拱形结构，即最初由石头或砖块构成的弧形结构。

由于本考点的前句话some of the world's finest...of Peru是进一步举例说明其前句话的：in the past, whole cities grew from the arduous task of cutting and piling stone upon stone. 可见，本考点的内容与此句无关。所以本考点只能与其后面的内容相关。因此，选项(C)是正确答案：列举一个在拱形结构被发明之前的建筑形式，这是对考点后面那句话内容的同义转述。

错误选项分析：

(A) To indicate that ~~the combined skeletons and skins~~ of the stone buildings of Machu Picchu... 删除线内容不是本段所讨论的问题，不用考虑。

(B) To indicate the ~~different kinds of stones~~ that had to be cut to build Machu Picchu. 删除线内容不是本段所讨论的问题，故可排除。

(D) To explain how ancient builders ~~reduced the amount of time~~ necessary to construct buildings from stone. 删除线内容在本段中没被提及，不用考虑。

12

定位句：A structural invention had to be made before the physical limitations of stone could be overcome and new architectural forms could be created. That invention was the arch, a curved structure originally made of separate stone or brick segments.

在原文中that invention (the arch) = a structural invention，即the arch 使新的建筑结构被创造出来。故选项(B)是正确答案：拱形结构的发明使新的建筑形式得到发展。

本题最容易被误选的是选项(A)。此选项的内容与原文叙述不符。原文为：The arch was used by the early cultures of the Mediterranean area chiefly for underground drains, but it was the **Romans** who first developed and used the arch extensively in **aboveground structures**. 即原文强调Romans是最早在地面建筑上使用arch的人。而选项(A)只说Romans是最早使用arch的人，与原文陈述内容不符，故错误。

13

However, some modern architectural designs, such as those using folded plates of concreter or air-inflated structures, are **again** unifying skeleton and skin.

逻辑点：however, again

however 要求后面的内容与前面的内容是对立的两个概念，again要求其后面的概念在前文中被提及。结合这两个逻辑点的要求，正确答案为第四个■。其前句话为：Of course in early architecture—such as igloos and adobe structures—there was no such equipment, and the skeleton and skin were often one. 这个句子中的early architecture 与however 后面some modern architectural designs相对立，且the skeleton and skin were often one 这个概念在unifying skeleton and skin这个概念前被提及。

14

提示句：Architecture uses forms and space to express cultural values.

(1)	✔	
(2)	✘	第二段结尾处的细节内容，与主旨内容关系不大。
(3)	✔	
(4)	✘	modern buildings tend to lack the beauty of ancient stone buildings此概念在原文中没被提及，必错。
(5)	✘	needing distinct "organ" systems in order to function此概念在原文没被提及，必错。
(6)	✔	

本文词汇总结

architecture	*n.*	建筑学
arduous	*adj.*	艰辛的，费力的
bend	*v.*	弯曲
client	*n.*	顾客
component	*n.*	成分，组件
contemporary	*adj.*	当代的，同时代的
curved	*adj.*	曲线的，弧形的
delight	*n.*	愉悦
devise	*v.*	设计
divert	*v.*	转移
dimensional	*adj.*	维的，维度的
ease	*n.*	容易
enrich	*v.*	使充实
extensively	*adv.*	广泛地；广大地
feasible	*adj.*	可行的，可能的
gravity	*n.*	重力，地心引力
horizontal	*adj.*	水平的
instinctively	*adv.*	本能地
permanence	*n.*	永久性
practical	*adj.*	实用的
progress	*v.*	进步
structure	*n.*	结构
symbolic	*adj.*	象征的
tension	*n.*	张力，拉力
utilize	*v.*	利用
vertical	*adj.*	垂直的
visual	*adj.*	视觉的
withstand	*v.*	抵挡，禁得起

Passage 2
THE LONG-TERM STABILITY OF ECOSYSTEMS

文章结构

标 题	生态系统的长期稳定性
第一段	植物群落的发展从先锋群落开始，经过演替群落，最后到顶级群落。
第二段	生态系统比个体物种更加稳定。
第三段	生态学家曾经认为，生态系统的稳定性取决于构成系统的物种的多样性。
第四段	但是，关于稳定性的定义，生态学家们存在分歧。
第五段	有时候，物种的多样性并不能保证生态系统的稳定性。
第六段	生态学家最想搞清楚的是，哪些因素影响生态系统的恢复力。
第七段	现在，许多生态学家认为，环境的多样性和可适应性而非物种的多样性决定了生态系统的稳定性。

题目解析

1

(C) specific

【考】particular = **specific**

【英】special or more than usual

【汉】*adj.* 特定的，特殊的

【预】distinct, exact, peculiar, special

【例】The computer program will be of **particular** interest to teachers.

2

NOT/EXCEPT题型

此题正确答案为选项(C)。

原文的最后一句话为：Climax communities themselves **change** but over periods of time greater than about 500 years. 而选项(C)为：The numbers of plants in them and the mix of species **do not change**. 这与原文的观点相反，为正确选项。

3

定位句：We can say that the properties of an ecosystem are more stable than the individual organisms that compose the ecosystem.

译文：我们可以认为，生态系统自身的性质比组成生态系统的单个生物体更为稳定。

X are more stable than Y <==> X change more slowly than Y，故本题正确答案为选项(A)：生态系统的性质比系统中个体的性质改变得慢。

4

定位句：They believed that the greater the diversity the more stable the ecosystem. Support for this idea came from the observation that long-lasting climax communities usually have more complex food webs and more species diversity than pioneer communities.

从此定位句可知：生态学家曾经认为，生态系统内部的多样性越强，这个生态系统就越稳定。支持这个观点的证据来源于他们对climax communities的观察。因此，本题正确答案为选项(B)。

5

定位句：The first problem is that ecologists do not all agree what "stability" means.

译文：首先，并不是所有的生态学家都赞同“稳定性”这个词的含义。

正确答案为选项(C)：生态学家们争论“稳定性”这个词的确切意思。...is debated = not all agree...

6

定位句：Stability can be defined as simply lack of change. In that case, the climax community would be considered the most stable, since, by definition, it changes the least over time. Alternatively, stability can be defined as the speed with which an ecosystem returns to a particular form following a major disturbance, such as a fire. This kind of stability is also called *resilience*. In that case, climax communities would be the most fragile and the *least* stable, since they can require hundreds of years to return to the climax state.

译文：稳定性可以简单地定义为缺乏变化。如果是这样的话，顶极群落将被视为最稳定的，因为根据定义，它们随着时间推移而变化的程度是最小的。另外，稳定性也可以定义为生态系统在经历了严重破坏（比如火灾）之后恢复原貌的速度。这种稳定性也被称做“弹性”。根据这种判断标准，顶极群落是最脆弱和最不稳定的，因为它们可能需要数百年时间才能恢复到顶级状态。

故本题正确答案为选项(B)：它们既可以是最稳定的，也可以是最不稳定的生物群落。与原文定位句为同义转述关系。

> **注意：**在原文中有最高级出现的地方往往是考点所在。

7

定位句：At least in temperate zones, maximum diversity is often found in mid-successional stages, not in the climax community. Once a redwood forest matures, for example, ...

译文：至少在温带地区，经常会在演替过程中发现最多的物种，而不是在顶极群落中。例如，红树林一旦成熟……

文章先提出温带地区（temperate zones）的情况，之后又用 redwood forest 举例说明，由此可推断出 redwood forest 应该在 temperate zones。因此，正确答案为选项(C)：它们生长在温带地区。

错误选项分析：

(A) They become less stable as they mature. 原文只是说在它们mature时，物种类别和个体数目会减少，与是否stable之间没有任何关系。

(B) They support many species when they reach climax. 原文没有指出他们reach climax时，物种类别减少。此选项中many species与之相反。

(D) They have reduced diversity during mid-successional stages. 原文没有给出它们在mid-successional 阶段时diversity的信息。

8

(B) ensure

【考】guarantee = **ensure**

【英】to give security to

【汉】*v.* 保证，担保

【预】assure, certify, secure, warrant, make certain

【例】They **guarantee** that the diamonds they supply are top quality.

9

定位句： A more complicated system is, in general, more likely than a simple system to break down.

译文： 总体来讲，一个复杂的系统要比一个简单的系统更容易遭受破坏。

由此可知，题干中阴影部分的句子在解释说明定位句，其中fifteen-speed racing bicycle = a more complicated system, a child's tricycle = a simple system。故本题答案为选项(A)：用日常生活中的例子解释一个关于生态系统稳定性的总体规律。

错误选项分析：

(B) To demonstrate that an understanding of stability in ecosystems can be applied to help understand ~~stability in other situations~~.

(C) To make a ~~comparison~~ that...

(D) To provide an example that ~~contradicts~~...

对于这三个选项，在读到删除线部分的内容时即可判断为错，因为这些概念均未被原文提及。

10

(C) loses significance

【英】If one thing **pales** in comparison with another, it is made to seem much less important, serious or good by it.

【预】lose color, be less important

11

<u>Many ecologists now think that the relative long-term stability of climax communities comes not from diversity but from the "patchiness" of the environment</u>❶; an environment❷ [that varies from place to place and supports more kinds of organisms than an environment that is uniform]❸.

句子成分分析：

❶ 句子主干

❷ 作"patchiness" of the environment中environment的同位语。

❸ 定语从句，修饰 ❷ environment。

错误选项讲解：

(A) the stability of environment is a result of diversity rather than(=**no**) patchiness. 与原文句子主干：the stability comes not from diversity but from patchiness所表达的意思完全相反，必错。

根据❸定语从句中的内容可知：patchy environment既varies from place to place,又supports more kinds of organisms。选项(B)中patchy environments do not often have high species diversity与原文表述内容相反，必错。

选项(C)中uniform environments cannot be climax communities这种观点在原文中完全没有被提及。因为原文强调的是stability与patchiness of environment的关系，而patchy environment与uniform environment相比更能supports more kinds of organisms，所以uniform environment与climax communities之间并没有关系。选项(C)在此两者之间强行建立关联，必定错误。

故本题正确答案为选项(D)。

12

(D) neighboring

【考】adjacent = **neighboring**

【考】adjacent = nearby

【英】not distant, immediately preceding or following

【汉】*adj.* 毗连的，临近的，接近的

【预】adjoining, close, near, next, bordering, beside

【例】Their house is **adjacent** to a wooded park.

13

In fact, damage to the environment by humans is often much more severe than damage by natural events and processes.

逻辑点：本题较特殊，其逻辑点在原文中第二个■后面的句子中的for example。

本题依据句义“事实上，人为原因对自然环境造成的损害要远远大于自然事件所造成的损害”，应该放在第二个■。因为第二个■后面的句子直接举例说火山爆发对环境造成的损害远远小于人为原因对环境造成的损害。

第一个■位于段首，多数情况下可以排除。

14

提示句：The process of succession and the stability of a climax community can change over time.

(1)	✘	The changes that occur in an ecosystem from the pioneer to the climax community...该内容原文没有提及，必错。
(2)	✘	该内容与原文矛盾，必错。
(3)	✔	
(4)	✔	
(5)	✔	
(6)	✘	...makes them resistant to destruction该内容原文没有提及，必错。

本文词汇总结

apparent	*adj.*	显然的，表面上的
associated	*adj.*	有联系的
complicated	*adj.*	复杂的
cumulative	*adj.*	积累的
destruction	*n.*	破坏，毁灭
disturbance	*n.*	干扰；骚乱
dominate	*v.*	控制，支配
ecosystem	*n.*	生态系统
entire	*adj.*	全部的
explosion	*n.*	爆发
extinct	*adj.*	灭绝的
fluid	*adj.*	流动的
fragile	*adj.*	脆弱的
guarantee	*v.*	保证，担保
intact	*adj.*	完整的
likewise	*adv.*	同样地，也
mature	*v.*	成熟
opposite	*adj.*	相反的，对面的
patchiness	*n.*	云斑；云斑状
pest	*n.*	害虫
pioneer	*n.*	先驱
relatively	*adv.*	相对地
resistance	*n.*	抵抗
severely	*adv.*	严重地
tolerate	*v.*	忍受
vacate	*v.*	空出

Passage 3

DEPLETION OF THE OGALLALA AQUIFER

文章结构

标 题	美国奥加拉拉地下蓄水层的枯竭
第一段	20世纪初期，美国奥加拉拉地下蓄水层被发现。
第二段	奥加拉拉地下蓄水层覆盖面积广，储水量大；但由于当地的半干旱气候，蓄水层的蓄水率已经减少。
第三段	现在，奥加拉拉蓄水层上面已经有十万余口井，为当地大面积的农作物和美国40%的肉用牛养殖供水。
第四段	由于大量地向外抽水，奥加拉拉蓄水层的水量急剧下降。
第五段	农民们对奥加拉拉蓄水层必然枯竭的命运持不同的态度。
第六段	为了缓解即将来临的水源危机，多种方案正在尝试之中，但灌溉水再也不会像以前那样充足了。

题目解析

1

定位句：This region has a semiarid climate, and for 50 years after its settlement, it supported a low-intensity agricultural economy of cattle ranching and wheat farming.

译文：这个区域位于半干旱气候区。人们在这里定居后的50年中，（仅仅）发展了以畜牧业和小麦种植为主的低密度农业经济。

选项(D)：在20世纪早期之前，High Plains上只有少量的耕种和放牧，与本句为同义转述关系，故正确。

2

本题正确答案为选项(B)。

(A)(D)选项出自原文的第一句话： The Ogallala aquifer is a sandstone formation that underlies some 583,000 square kilometers of land extending from northwestern Texas to southern South Dakota. 选项(C)出自原文第二句话： Water from rains and melting snows has been accumulating in the Ogallala for the past 30,000 years.

3

原句逻辑关系：让步转折关系（but）

Estimates indicate that the aquifer contains enough water to fill Lake Huron❶, **but** unfortunately, under the semiarid climatic conditions [that presently exist in the region] ❸, rates of addition to the aquifer are minimal❷, amounting to about half a centimeter a year.

❶ 句子主干

❷ 句子主干，并且是原句强调的重心。

❸ 定语从句，修饰 semiarid climatic conditions。

解题步骤一：

选项(A) despite和选项(B) although都表示让步转折关系，可以保留。但(C)、(D)两选项均不含让步转折关系，故先可排除。

解题步骤二：

原文主要强调内容：rates of addition to the aquifer是少量的（minimal）。选项(A) rates of water addition = rates of addition to the aquifer, very small = minimal与原文强调内容相同。而选项(B) accumulate enough water 与原文强调内容相反，错误。

故本题正确答案为选项(A)。

4

(D) subsequent

【考】ensue = follow

【考】ensue = result

【英】to come at a later time; to happen as a result

【汉】*v.* 跟着发生，接着发生

【预】come next, derive, proceed, result, stem

【例】When the news broke, a long period of chaos **ensued**.

注意：将ensue 与 ensure (保证，确保) 区分开。

5

定位句：The ensuing rapid expansion of irrigation agriculture, especially from the 1950s onward, transformed the economy of the region. More than 100,000 wells now tap the Ogallala. Modern irrigation devices, each capable of spraying 4.5 million liters of water a day, have produced a landscape dominated by geometric patterns of circular green islands of crops. Ogallala water has enabled the High Plains region to supply significant amounts of the cotton, sorghum, wheat, and corn grown in the United States. In addition, 40 percent of American grain-fed beef cattle are fattened here.

译文：灌溉农业的迅速扩张，特别是20世纪50年代之后，改变了这一地区的经济。目前人们已经在奥加拉拉地区共开凿了十万多口井。日喷水量达到450万升的现代灌溉设备使该地区形成了一个圆形绿岛作物的景观。奥加拉拉蓄水层使北美大平原地区能够为美国提供充足的棉花、高粱、小麦和玉米。此外，美国40%谷物饲养的肉牛在这里被育肥。

In addition表示其后面的内容是对前句内容的进一步补充说明。前句话在讲Ogallala water对high Plains地区有好处，即解释它如何改变这个地区的经济。而40 percent of American grain-fed beef cattle are fattened here 也是一个正面的支持性信息，说明是Ogallala water 对

high Plains 地区的另外一个好处。故正确答案为选项(C)：为解释来自奥加拉拉的水如何改变了大平原经济提供另外一个例子。

错误选项分析：

(A) To suggest that crop cultivation is not ~~the most important~~ part of...

(B) To indicate that not all economic activity in the High Plains is ~~dependent on irrigation~~

(D) To ~~contrast~~...

删除线部分在原文没有提及，均错误。

6

(C) unlike anything in the past

【考】unprecedented = initial

【考】unprecedented = new

【考】unprecedented = novel

【考】unprecedented = unheard of

【考】unprecedented = unique

【英】not done or experienced before

【汉】*adj.* 无先例的，空前的

【预】extraordinary, original, remarkable

【例】The team has enjoyed **unprecedented** success this year.

7

(D) almost

【考】virtually = actually

【考】virtually = in fact

【考】virtually = nearly

【考】virtually = **almost**

【英】very nearly, almost entirely

【汉】*adv.* 实际上，事实上，几乎

【预】practically, in essence

【例】We spent **virtually** all day shopping.

8

NOT/ EXCEPT题型

选项(A)在原文中未被提及，故为正确选项。

定位句：This unprecedented development of a finite groundwater resource with an almost negligible natural recharge rate—that is, virtually no natural water source to replenish the water supply—has caused water tables in the region to fall drastically. [选项(B)出处] In the 1930s, wells encountered plentiful water at a depth of about 15 meters; currently, they must be dug to depths of 45 to 60 meters or more. [选项(C)出处] In places, the water table is declining at a rate of a meter a year, necessitating the periodic deepening of wells and the use of ever-more-powerful pumps. [选项(D)出处] It is estimated that at current withdrawal rates, much of the aquifer will run dry within 40 years.

9

定位句：The situation is most critical in Texas, where the climate is driest, the greatest amount of water is being pumped, and the aquifer contains the least water.

译文：这种现象在气候最干旱的得克萨斯州尤为严重，在这里最大量的水被从地下抽出，但这个地区蓄水层的含水量却是最少的。

原文最高级处常设为考点。选项(C)：随着Ogallala蓄水层的逐渐干枯，Texas被认为将会面临最严重的供水危机，与定位句陈述内容一致，the worst对应原文的most critical，为正确答案。

10

(C) unavoidable

【考】inevitable = **unavoidable**

【考】inevitable = without exception

【英】sure to happen

【汉】*adj.* 不可避免的

【预】certain, fixed, sure

【例】Some criticism was **inevitable**.

11

定位句：The incentive of the farmers who wish to conserve water is reduced by their knowledge that **many of their neighbors are profiting by using great amounts of water**...

译文：当那些想节水的农民得知许多邻居通过大量耗水种植而盈利的时候，他们节水的动机减弱了。

本题为细节题。选项(B)：种植大量耗水农作物的农场主得到了更高的利润，与本句为同义转述关系，为正确答案。

12

定位句：Unfortunately, the cost of water obtained through any of these schemes would increase pumping costs at least tenfold, making the cost of irrigated agricultural products from the region uncompetitive on the national and international markets.

本句强调，水的成本的上升导致费用的上升，从而使农产品成本上升，进而使农产品失去在国内及国际市场上的竞争力。选项(B)：增长的灌溉成本会使农产品的价格过高，与本句强调内容一致，为正确答案。

13

But even if uncooperative farmers **were** to join in the conservation efforts, this **would** only delay the depletion of the aquifer.

本句为虚拟语气，强调“即使这些不愿意合作的农民参与到节约用水的努力中，这也仅仅是延迟蓄水层的枯竭而已”。这要求本句的前文应提过这些内容：不愿意合作的农民（uncooperative farmers）、愿意合作的农民（farmers who wish to conserve water）及蓄水层的不断枯竭。而能够满足这些条件的位置只有第三个■的位置。

故本题正确答案为第三个■。

14

提示句：The Ogallala aquifer is a large underground source of water in the High Plains region of the United States.

(1)	✔	第二、三段主旨内容。
(2)	✘	该内容原文没有提及，必错。
(3)	✔	第四段主旨内容。
(4)	✘	此内容在原文的细节例子部分出现，不需做任何考虑，必错。
(5)	✘	原文中没有这两项措施之间的比较，必错。
(6)	✔	第六段主旨内容。

本文词汇总结

aquifer	*n.*	蓄水层
acreage	*n.*	面积
capable	*adj.*	有能力的
conserve	*v.*	保存；节约
critical	*adj.*	严重的
cultivation	*n.*	栽培
depletion	*n.*	消耗；耗尽，枯竭
drastically	*adv.*	急剧地
drought	*n.*	干旱
entire	*adj.*	整个的
finite	*adj.*	有限的
genetic	*adj.*	基因的
geometric	*adj.*	几何的
grandiose	*adj.*	宏伟的
incentive	*n.*	动机
inevitable	*adj.*	必然的，不可避免的
initial	*adj.*	最初的
inject	*v.*	注入
irrigation	*n.*	灌溉
periodic	*adj.*	周期的
predictable	*adj.*	可预测的
presently	*adv.*	目前
rancher	*n.*	牧场主
replenish	*v.*	补充，重新装满
scheme	*n.*	方案，计划
spray	*v.*	喷射
subsequent	*adj.*	随后发生的
tenfold	*adj.*	十倍的